# Crochet Animals Guidebook

## Make 12 Cute Furry Friends and 35 Trendy Clothes and Accessories

*Aliyah M Kane*

# THIS BOOK BELONGS TO
## *The Library of*

..................................................................

..................................................................

# ©COPYRIGHT 2023
# ALL RIGHTS RESERVED

The content contained within this book may not be reproduced, duplicated, or transmitted without direct written permission from the author or the publisher. Under no circumstances will any blame or legal responsibility be held against the publisher, or author, for any damages, reparation, or monetary loss due to the information contained within this book. Either directly or indirectly.

**Legal Notice:**
This book is copyright protected. This book is only for personal use. You cannot amend, distribute, sell, use, quote, or paraphrase any part, or the content within this book, without the consent of the author or publisher.

**Disclaimer Notice:**
Please note the information contained within this document is for educational and entertainment purposes only. All effort has been executed to present accurate, up-to-date, and reliable, complete information. No warranties of any kind are declared or implied. Readers acknowledge that the author is not engaging in the rendering of legal, financial, medical, or professional advice. The content within this book has been derived from various sources. Please consult a licensed professional before attempting any techniques outlined in this book. By reading this document, the reader agrees that under no circumstances is the author responsible for any losses, direct or indirect, which are incurred as a result of the use of the information contained within this document, including, but not limited to — errors, omissions, or inaccuracies.

# Table of Contents

SUMMARY

    My animals — 26

    To the forest! — 28

        The bear — 29

        The raccoon — 34

        The fox — 39

        The deer — 42

        The wolf — 47

    In love — 50

        The koala — 51

        The panda — 54

    Three little pigs — 59

        The chef — 60

        The butcher — 63

        The junior chef — 66

    Rabbit's little family — 71

        The mummy bunny and her baby — 72

    My animal carry-all — 77

    Patterns — 80

    Yarn — 193

    Tables — 198

## SUMMARY

**The Joy of Crafting Furry Friends in Crochet**: The Joy of Crafting Furry Friends in Crochet is a comprehensive guidebook that delves into the world of creating adorable and huggable stuffed animals using the art of crochet. This book is a must-have for both beginners and experienced crocheters who have a passion for creating unique and personalized toys.

The author, a seasoned crochet artist and enthusiast, takes readers on a journey through the process of designing and crafting various furry friends, from cute little kittens to playful puppies and everything in between. With step-by-step instructions and detailed patterns, this book provides all the necessary tools and techniques to bring these lovable creatures to life.

One of the highlights of this book is the emphasis on customization and personalization. The author encourages readers to add their own creative touches to each project, allowing them to create truly one-of-a-kind toys. Whether it's choosing different colors, adding accessories, or experimenting with different stitches, this book empowers readers to unleash their creativity and make each furry friend truly unique.

In addition to the patterns and instructions, The Joy of Crafting Furry Friends in Crochet also provides valuable tips and tricks for working with different types of yarn, selecting the right crochet hooks, and achieving the perfect tension. The author's expertise shines through as she shares her insights and advice, making this book not only a source of inspiration but also a practical resource for crocheters of all skill levels.

Furthermore, this book goes beyond just the technical aspects of crochet. It explores the joy and satisfaction that comes from creating something with your own hands and the emotional connection that can be formed with these handmade toys. The author shares heartwarming stories and anecdotes about the joy and happiness that her creations have brought to others, reminding readers of the power of handmade gifts and the impact they can have on both the creator and the recipient.

The Joy of Crafting Furry Friends in Crochet is not just a book about crochet; it is a celebration of creativity, imagination, and the joy of crafting. Whether you're a seasoned crocheter looking for new projects or a beginner eager to learn the art of crochet, this book is sure to inspire and delight. So grab your crochet hooks, choose your favorite yarn, and get ready to embark on a delightful journey of creating furry friends that will bring joy and warmth to your heart.

**Materials and Tools in Crochet**: What You'll Need for This Adventure: When embarking on the adventure of crochet, it is essential to have the right materials and tools at your disposal. These items will not only make your crochet journey more enjoyable but also ensure that you can create beautiful and intricate designs with ease.

First and foremost, you will need yarn. Yarn comes in various colors, textures, and thicknesses, allowing you to choose the perfect one for your project. It is important to consider the type of yarn that is suitable for the item you are crocheting. For example, if you are making a cozy blanket, you may want to opt for a soft and warm yarn, while a lightweight and breathable yarn would be ideal for a summer top.

In addition to yarn, you will also need crochet hooks. Crochet hooks come in different sizes, ranging from small to large, and are typically made of metal, plastic, or wood. The size of the crochet hook you choose will depend on the thickness of your yarn and the desired tension of your stitches. It is advisable to have a variety of crochet hooks in your collection to accommodate different projects and yarn weights.

Another essential tool in crochet is a pair of scissors. Scissors are used to cut the yarn and trim any loose ends. It is important to have a sharp pair of scissors that can easily cut through the yarn without fraying or damaging it.

Furthermore, you will need a tapestry needle or yarn needle. These needles have large eyes and blunt tips, making it easier to weave in loose ends and sew pieces together. They are particularly useful when finishing off your crochet projects and ensuring that all loose ends are neatly tucked away.

To keep track of your progress and count stitches, stitch markers are indispensable. Stitch markers are small, removable rings or clips that can be placed on your work to mark specific stitches or sections. They help you keep track of where you are in your pattern and prevent any mistakes or confusion.

Lastly, a measuring tape or ruler is essential for ensuring that your crochet project is the correct size. This is particularly important when making garments or items that need to fit a specific measurement. A measuring tape or ruler will help you accurately measure your work and make any necessary adjustments.

In conclusion, having the right materials and tools is crucial for a successful crochet adventure. Yarn, crochet hooks, scissors, tapestry needles, stitch markers, and measuring tape are all essential items that will make your crochet journey more enjoyable and help you create beautiful and intricate designs.

**Understanding the Basics of Amigurumi in Crochet**: Amigurumi is a popular Japanese crochet technique that involves creating small stuffed animals or dolls using yarn and a crochet hook. It has gained a lot of popularity in recent years, as it allows crafters to create adorable and customizable toys.

To get started with amigurumi, it's important to have a basic understanding of crochet techniques. If you're new to crochet, it's a good idea to familiarize yourself with the basic stitches such as chain stitch, single crochet, double crochet, and slip stitch. These stitches will form the foundation of your amigurumi projects.

Once you have a grasp of the basic stitches, you can start working on your first amigurumi project. The first step is to choose a pattern. There are countless amigurumi patterns available online, ranging from simple designs to more complex ones. It's a good idea to start with a beginner-friendly pattern that includes detailed instructions and step-by-step photos.

When it comes to choosing yarn for your amigurumi, it's best to opt for a medium-weight yarn that is soft and easy to work with. Acrylic yarn is a popular choice for amigurumi projects, as it is affordable and comes in a wide range of colors. You'll also need a crochet hook that is appropriate for the yarn you're using. The size of the hook will depend on the thickness of the yarn and the desired size of your finished amigurumi.

Once you have your pattern, yarn, and crochet hook ready, it's time to start crocheting. The first step is to create a magic ring, which will serve as the starting point for your amigurumi. This technique allows you to create a tight and seamless circle, which is essential for creating the head or body of your amigurumi.

From there, you'll follow the pattern instructions to create the different parts of your amigurumi, such as the head, body, arms, and legs. Each part is typically crocheted in the round, using a combination of single crochet and increases or decreases to shape the piece. It's important to pay attention to the pattern instructions and stitch counts to ensure that your amigurumi turns out the way you want it to.

Once you have all the parts crocheted, it's time to assemble your amigurumi. This involves sewing the different parts together using a yarn needle.

**Selecting the Perfect Yarns for Furry Textures in Crochet**: When it comes to creating crochet projects with furry textures, selecting the perfect yarn is crucial. The right yarn can make all the difference in achieving the desired fluffy and soft texture. There are several factors to consider when choosing yarns for furry textures in crochet, including fiber content, weight, and texture.

One of the most important considerations is the fiber content of the yarn. For furry textures, yarns made from animal fibers such as mohair, alpaca, or angora are ideal. These fibers have a natural fluffiness and softness that can create a realistic and luxurious furry effect. Mohair, in particular, is known for its long, silky fibers that mimic the look of fur. Alpaca and angora fibers are also incredibly soft and have a natural halo that adds to the furry texture.

Another factor to consider is the weight of the yarn. Furry textures are best achieved with bulky or super bulky weight yarns. These thicker yarns create a denser fabric that can hold the fluffiness and volume needed for a furry texture. The extra thickness also helps to hide any gaps or holes in the stitches, resulting in a more cohesive and realistic look.

Texture is another important aspect to consider when selecting yarns for furry textures. Yarns with a brushed or boucle texture are ideal for creating a furry effect. Brushed yarns have loose fibers that are brushed out to create a fluffy appearance, while boucle yarns have loops that add texture and dimension. Both types of yarns can create a realistic and soft furry texture in crochet projects.

In addition to these considerations, it's also important to think about the color of the yarn. Choosing yarns in natural or neutral colors can enhance the realistic look of the furry texture. Browns, grays, and creams are popular choices for creating fur-like textures. However, don't be afraid to experiment with different colors to create unique and whimsical furry textures.

When selecting yarns for furry textures in crochet, it's always a good idea to swatch and test different yarns before starting a project. This allows you to see how the yarn behaves and how the furry texture will look in your chosen stitch pattern. It's also important to consider the care instructions for the yarn, as some furry yarns may require special handling or gentle washing to maintain their texture.

In conclusion, selecting the perfect yarns for furry textures in crochet involves considering the fiber content, weight, texture, and color.

**Essential Stitches and Techniques for Animal Patterns in Crochet:**

This book is a comprehensive guide that provides detailed instructions and step-by-step tutorials on how to create various animal patterns using crochet techniques.

Crochet is a popular craft that involves creating fabric by interlocking loops of yarn or thread using a crochet hook. It is a versatile and creative art form that allows individuals to bring their imagination to life through the creation of various items, including adorable animal patterns.

The book begins by introducing the basic stitches and techniques that are essential for creating animal patterns in crochet. It covers the fundamental stitches such as chain stitch, single crochet, double crochet, and treble crochet, providing clear explanations and illustrations to ensure that even beginners can easily grasp the concepts.

Once the basics are covered, the book delves into more advanced stitches and techniques that are specific to creating animal patterns. It explores techniques such as increasing and decreasing stitches, which are crucial for shaping the different parts of an animal's body. It also covers techniques like color changes and working in the round, which are essential for adding intricate details and creating seamless patterns.

The book then proceeds to showcase a wide range of animal patterns that can be created using the stitches and techniques taught earlier. From cute and cuddly teddy bears to majestic lions and graceful dolphins, the book provides patterns for a variety of animals, catering to different skill levels and preferences.

Each pattern is accompanied by detailed instructions, including stitch counts, color changes, and any special techniques required. The book also includes clear and colorful photographs of the finished projects, allowing readers to visualize the end result and gain inspiration for their own creations.

In addition to the patterns, the book also includes helpful tips and tricks from experienced crocheters, providing valuable insights and guidance to readers. These tips cover topics such as yarn selection, gauge, and finishing techniques, ensuring that readers have all the necessary information to successfully complete their animal patterns.

Overall, this book is a comprehensive and user-friendly guide that equips readers with the knowledge and skills needed to create beautiful and lifelike animal patterns using crochet. Whether you are a beginner or an experienced crocheter, this book is a valuable resource that will inspire and guide you in your crochet journey.

**Pattern and Assembly Instructions in Crochet:** A comprehensive guide on how to create a crochet project using a specific pattern and assembly instructions.

Crochet is a popular craft that involves creating fabric by interlocking loops of yarn or thread using a crochet hook. It is a versatile and creative hobby that allows individuals to make a wide range of items, from clothing and accessories to home decor and toys.

When starting a crochet project, it is essential to have a pattern and assembly instructions to guide you through the process. The pattern provides a blueprint for the project, detailing the stitches, techniques, and measurements required to create the desired item. Assembly instructions, on the other hand, explain how to put the different components of the project together to achieve the final result.

To begin, you will need to gather all the necessary materials for your crochet project. This typically includes yarn or thread in the desired color and weight, a crochet hook that matches the recommended size in the pattern, and any additional materials such as buttons or zippers if required. It is important to choose the right materials to ensure that your finished project turns out as intended.

Once you have your materials ready, you can start by reading through the pattern carefully. The pattern will usually include a list of abbreviations and special stitches used throughout the project, so it is essential to familiarize yourself with these before you begin. It is also a good idea to read any notes or tips provided by the pattern designer, as they may offer valuable insights or suggestions for modifications.

Next, you will need to follow the pattern instructions step by step. This may involve creating a foundation chain, working rows or rounds of stitches, and shaping the fabric as required. It is crucial to pay attention to the stitch counts and measurements provided in the pattern to ensure that your project turns out the correct size and shape. If you are unsure about any part of the pattern, it is always a good idea to consult online tutorials or seek guidance from experienced crocheters.

Once you have completed all the individual components of your project, it is time to assemble them according to the provided instructions. This may involve sewing or attaching different pieces together, adding embellishments, or finishing edges. Assembly instructions are typically written in a clear and concise manner, guiding you through each step of the process. It is important to follow these instructions carefully to achieve a polished and professional-looking finished product.

Finally, after completing the assembly, you can add any final touches or embellishments to your crochet project.

**Tips for Fluffy Texture and Character Details in Crochet**: When it comes to crochet, achieving a fluffy texture and adding character details to your projects can really elevate the final result. Whether you're working on a cozy blanket, a cute amigurumi toy, or a stylish accessory, these tips will help you create a beautiful and unique piece.

To start, selecting the right yarn is crucial for achieving a fluffy texture. Opt for yarns that are specifically labeled as "fluffy" or "chunky." These yarns are typically made with fibers that have a higher loft, resulting in a soft and fluffy appearance. Mohair, alpaca, and angora blends are great options to consider. Additionally, choosing yarns with a brushed or boucle texture can also add to the fluffiness of your project.

Another technique to create a fluffy texture is to use larger crochet hooks. By using a hook size that is larger than what is recommended for the yarn, you can create looser stitches that allow the yarn to puff up and create a fluffy effect. Experiment with different hook sizes to find the right balance between stitch definition and fluffiness.

When it comes to adding character details to your crochet projects, there are several techniques you can employ. One popular method is using different stitch patterns to create texture and dimension. For example, using popcorn stitches, bobbles, or clusters can add a three-dimensional element to your work. These stitches create small raised bumps or balls that give your project a unique and interesting look.

Additionally, incorporating colorwork can also add character to your crochet projects. Introducing different colors through stripes, color changes, or intricate patterns can make your project visually appealing and eye-catching. Consider using variegated yarns or creating your own color combinations to make your project truly one-of-a-kind.

Furthermore, adding embellishments such as buttons, beads, or embroidery can enhance the character of your crochet piece. These small details can bring your project to life and make it stand out. Sewing on buttons as eyes for an amigurumi toy, adding beads to a scarf, or embroidering flowers onto a blanket are just a few examples of how you can incorporate these details.

Lastly, paying attention to finishing touches can make a big difference in the overall appearance of your crochet project. Blocking your finished piece can help to even out stitches and give it a more polished look. Additionally, weaving in ends neatly and securely ensures that your project maintains its shape and durability over time.

**Adapting Patterns for Different Animal Sizes in Crochet:** When it comes to crochet patterns, one size does not fit all, especially when it comes to creating items for different animal sizes. Adapting patterns to accommodate the varying sizes of animals is an essential skill for any crochet enthusiast who wants to create custom-made items for their furry friends.

The first step in adapting a crochet pattern for different animal sizes is to understand the measurements of the specific animal you are crocheting for. This includes the length from the neck to the tail, the circumference of the neck, chest, and waist, as well as the size of the legs and paws. By taking accurate measurements, you can ensure that the finished crochet item will fit the animal comfortably.

Once you have the measurements, the next step is to adjust the pattern accordingly. This can be done by modifying the number of stitches and rows in the pattern to match the animal's size. For example, if the original pattern calls for 20 stitches for a small dog, you may need to increase the number of stitches to 30 for a larger dog. Similarly, you may need to add or subtract rows to achieve the desired length or width of the item.

In addition to adjusting the stitch count and rows, it is also important to consider the type of yarn and crochet hook size used in the pattern. Thicker yarn and larger hooks will create a larger finished item, while thinner yarn and smaller hooks will result in a smaller item. By selecting the appropriate yarn and hook size, you can further customize the crochet item to fit the animal's size.

Another aspect to consider when adapting patterns for different animal sizes is the overall design and shape of the item. For example, a sweater pattern designed for a small dog may need to be modified to have a longer body and wider chest for a larger dog. Similarly, a hat pattern may need to be adjusted to have a larger circumference to fit a bigger head. By understanding the anatomy and proportions of the animal, you can make these necessary modifications to ensure a proper fit.

It is also worth noting that some patterns may require additional adjustments, such as adding or subtracting stitches for shaping or incorporating increases and decreases to achieve the desired shape. These modifications may vary depending on the specific pattern and animal size, so it is important to carefully read and understand the pattern instructions before making any adjustments.

In conclusion, adapting crochet patterns for different animal sizes requires careful consideration of measurements, stitch count, yarn, hook size, and overall design.

**Embellishing with Beads, Sequins, and Other Trims in Crochet:** Embellishing with beads, sequins, and other trims in crochet is a creative and exciting way to add a touch of glamour and uniqueness to your crochet projects. Whether you're working on a garment, accessory, or home decor item, incorporating these embellishments can elevate your crochet work to a whole new level.

Beads are a popular choice for crochet embellishments as they come in a wide variety of colors, shapes, and sizes. They can be used to create intricate patterns, add texture, or simply add a pop of color to your crochet piece. Beads can be threaded onto the yarn before you start crocheting, or they can be added individually using a crochet hook. The latter method allows for more flexibility in terms of placement and design.

Sequins, on the other hand, are small, shiny discs that can be sewn onto your crochet work to create a dazzling effect. They are available in various shapes, such as round, square, or star-shaped, and can be found in a range of colors and finishes. Sequins can be sewn onto your crochet piece using a needle and thread, or they can be attached using a crochet hook. They can be used sparingly for a subtle sparkle or applied generously for a more dramatic look.

In addition to beads and sequins, there are numerous other trims that can be used to embellish your crochet projects. These include ribbons, lace, pom-poms, tassels, and even feathers. Ribbons can be woven through the stitches of your crochet work to create a decorative border or used as ties for closures. Lace can be sewn onto your crochet piece to add a delicate and feminine touch. Pom-poms and tassels can be attached to the corners or edges of your crochet work to create a playful and whimsical look. Feathers can be incorporated into your crochet projects to add a bohemian or tribal vibe.

When embellishing with beads, sequins, and other trims in crochet, it's important to consider the overall design and aesthetic of your project. You want the embellishments to enhance the crochet work rather than overpower it. It's also important to choose materials that are suitable for the type of crochet yarn you're using. For example, if you're working with a delicate lace-weight yarn, you may want to opt for lightweight beads and sequins to avoid weighing down the fabric.

**Techniques for Personalizing Facial Features in Crochet**:

Crocheting is a versatile and creative craft that allows individuals to create unique and personalized items. One popular aspect of crochet is the ability to personalize facial features on dolls, amigurumi, and other crocheted creations. Adding facial features can bring a sense of life and character to these creations, making them truly one-of-a-kind.

There are several techniques that can be used to personalize facial features in crochet. One common method is the use of embroidery. Embroidery allows for intricate and detailed facial features to be added to crocheted items. This technique involves using a needle and thread to create stitches that form the desired facial features, such as eyes, eyebrows, and mouths. Embroidery can be done using various stitches, such as satin stitch, backstitch, or French knots, depending on the desired effect.

Another technique for personalizing facial features in crochet is the use of appliqué. Appliqué involves attaching pre-made fabric or crocheted pieces to the crocheted item to create the desired facial features. This technique allows for more three-dimensional and textured facial features, such as noses or ears, to be added. Appliqué can be done using a variety of materials, such as felt, fabric, or even crocheted pieces, and can be attached using sewing or crochet techniques.

Additionally, crochet enthusiasts can use the technique of surface crochet to personalize facial features. Surface crochet involves working stitches directly onto the surface of the crocheted item, creating raised or textured designs. This technique can be used to add details such as freckles, dimples, or even facial hair to crocheted creations. Surface crochet can be done using a crochet hook or a tapestry needle, depending on the desired effect and the thickness of the yarn being used.

When personalizing facial features in crochet, it is important to consider the overall design and style of the crocheted item. The size and shape of the facial features should be proportionate to the size of the item and should complement its overall aesthetic. It is also important to consider the materials being used, as different yarns and fabrics can create different effects and textures.

In conclusion, personalizing facial features in crochet can add a unique and individual touch to crocheted creations. Techniques such as embroidery, appliqué, and surface crochet can be used to create intricate and detailed facial features that bring these creations to life.

**Cleaning and Maintenance Tips in Crochet:** Cleaning and maintaining crochet items is essential to keep them looking their best and prolong their lifespan. Whether you have a delicate lace doily or a cozy afghan, following these tips will help you keep your crochet creations in pristine condition.

First and foremost, it is important to read and follow the care instructions provided with the yarn you used for your crochet project. Different types of yarn require different cleaning methods, so it is crucial to understand the specific requirements for your particular item. Some yarns may be machine washable, while others may need to be hand washed or dry cleaned. By adhering to the recommended care instructions, you can avoid damaging or shrinking your crochet piece.

For machine washable crochet items, it is generally best to place them in a mesh laundry bag or pillowcase to protect them from getting tangled or stretched during the washing process. Use a gentle cycle with cold water and a mild detergent specifically designed for delicate fabrics. Avoid using bleach or harsh chemicals, as they can weaken the fibers and cause discoloration.

When hand washing crochet items, fill a basin or sink with lukewarm water and add a small amount of mild detergent. Gently agitate the water to create suds, then submerge the crochet piece and let it soak for a few minutes. Avoid rubbing or wringing the item, as this can cause it to lose its shape. After soaking, rinse the item thoroughly with cool water until all the soap is removed. To remove excess water, gently press the item between clean towels or roll it up and squeeze out the water. Avoid twisting or wringing the item, as this can cause it to stretch or become misshapen.

Drying crochet items properly is crucial to prevent them from losing their shape or becoming misshapen. Lay the item flat on a clean, dry towel or blocking mat, shaping it to its original dimensions. Avoid hanging crochet items to dry, as this can cause them to stretch or sag. Allow the item to air dry completely before storing or using it again.

In addition to regular cleaning, it is important to store crochet items properly to prevent damage. Fold or roll the item gently and place it in a clean, dry storage container or bag. Avoid storing crochet items in direct sunlight or in areas with high humidity, as this can cause fading, discoloration, or mold growth.

**Storing to Retain Shape and Texture in Crochet**: When it comes to crochet, one of the challenges that many crafters face is how to store their finished projects in order to retain their shape and texture. Crochet items, especially those made with delicate yarns or intricate stitch patterns, can easily lose their form if not stored properly. However, with a few simple techniques and tips, you can ensure that your crochet creations stay in pristine condition for years to come.

First and foremost, it is important to choose the right storage method for your crochet items. Avoid folding or cramming them into tight spaces, as this can cause the stitches to become misshapen or stretched out. Instead, opt for storing your projects flat or hanging them up. Flat storage is ideal for larger items such as blankets or shawls, while hanging storage works well for smaller items like scarves or hats.

When storing your crochet items flat, make sure to use acid-free tissue paper or cotton fabric to protect them from dust and moisture. Place a layer of tissue paper or fabric between each item to prevent them from sticking together or getting tangled. If you have multiple layers of crochet items, consider placing a piece of cardboard or foam board between each layer to provide additional support and prevent any weight from pressing down on the stitches.

If you choose to hang your crochet items, use padded hangers or fabric loops to avoid stretching or distorting the shape of the garment. Avoid using wire hangers, as they can leave creases or indentations on the fabric. Additionally, make sure to hang your items in a cool, dry place away from direct sunlight to prevent any fading or damage to the yarn.

In addition to proper storage techniques, there are a few other tips and tricks that can help retain the shape and texture of your crochet projects. One such tip is to block your items before storing them. Blocking involves wetting the crochet piece, shaping it to the desired dimensions, and allowing it to dry in that shape. This helps to even out the stitches and give the item a more polished and professional look. Blocking can be done using blocking mats, pins, and a spray bottle of water. Once the item is dry, it can be stored using the aforementioned methods.

Another helpful tip is to avoid storing your crochet items in plastic bags or containers. While these may seem like a convenient option for keeping your projects safe from dust and pests, they can actually trap moisture and cause the yarn to become damp or moldy.

**Repairing Wear and Tear in Crochet:** Crochet is a popular craft that involves creating fabric by interlocking loops of yarn with a crochet hook. Over time, crocheted items may experience wear and tear due to regular use or mishandling. However, there are several techniques and methods that can be employed to repair and restore crocheted pieces, ensuring their longevity and continued use.

One common issue with crocheted items is the occurrence of holes or tears. To repair these, you will need a crochet hook and matching yarn. Start by examining the damaged area and determining the extent of the damage. If the hole is small, you can simply use the crochet hook to weave the yarn through the existing stitches around the hole, creating new stitches to close the gap. This technique is known as "darning" and is commonly used for repairing small holes in crochet.

For larger tears or holes, you may need to employ a more extensive repair method. Begin by unraveling the damaged area until you reach the last intact row of stitches. Then, using the crochet hook, carefully recreate the missing stitches by working your way back up to the current row. This process requires a bit more skill and patience, as you will need to match the tension and stitch pattern of the original piece. However, with practice, you can achieve a seamless repair that is virtually undetectable.

Another common issue with crocheted items is the occurrence of loose or unraveled stitches. This can happen over time due to the natural stretching and pulling of the fabric. To fix loose stitches, start by identifying the affected area and gently pulling on the loose yarn to tighten the stitch. If the stitch is too loose to be fixed by simply tightening, you can use a crochet hook to weave the loose yarn back into the surrounding stitches, securing it in place.

In some cases, crocheted items may also experience color fading or discoloration. This can be caused by exposure to sunlight or improper washing techniques. To restore the color of your crocheted piece, you can try using fabric dyes specifically designed for yarn or fabric. Follow the instructions provided with the dye to ensure proper application and color restoration. It is important to note that not all yarns are suitable for dyeing, so it is recommended to check the yarn label or consult with a professional before attempting to dye your crocheted item.

In addition to repairing wear and tear, it is also important to take preventive measures to prolong the lifespan of your crocheted items.

**Designing Your Own Animal Characters in Crochet**: Designing your own animal characters in crochet is a fun and creative way to express your love for both crochet and animals. Whether you are a beginner or an experienced crocheter, this activity allows you to unleash your imagination and create unique and personalized animal characters that reflect your style and personality.

To start designing your own animal characters, you will need some basic crochet skills and knowledge of different crochet stitches. If you are new to crochet, there are plenty of online tutorials and resources available that can help you learn the basics. Once you have a good understanding of crochet techniques, you can begin exploring different animal patterns and designs to get inspiration for your own creations.

One of the first steps in designing your own animal characters is deciding on the type of animal you want to create. You can choose from a wide range of options, including domestic animals like cats and dogs, farm animals like cows and pigs, or even exotic animals like elephants and giraffes. Consider your own interests and preferences when selecting the animal, as this will make the design process more enjoyable and personal.

After selecting the animal, you can start sketching out your design on paper. This step is crucial as it allows you to visualize your creation and make any necessary adjustments before starting the crochet process. Pay attention to the proportions and details of the animal, such as the shape of the head, body, and limbs. You can also add unique features or accessories to make your character stand out.

Once you have finalized your design, it's time to gather the necessary materials and start crocheting. Choose a suitable yarn color that matches the animal you are creating, and make sure to select the appropriate crochet hook size for the yarn thickness. Follow your sketch as a guide and start crocheting the different parts of the animal, such as the head, body, and limbs. You can use different crochet stitches to add texture and detail to your creation.

As you crochet each part, remember to stuff them with fiberfill or stuffing material to give your animal character a three-dimensional shape. This will make your creation more realistic and huggable. Once all the parts are crocheted and stuffed, you can sew them together using a yarn needle and secure any loose ends.

To add the finishing touches to your animal character, you can embroider or sew on details like eyes, nose, and mouth. You can also use additional yarn or felt to create accessories like hats, scarves, or bows to give your character a unique.

# *My animals*

# To the forest!

# The bear

*A short break…*

*Never without my hat !*

*...by the fire*

*My little backpack*

# The raccoon

*Climbing trees*

*Mischievous look*

*Gathering nuts*

*Quick drying !*

# The fox

# *The deer*

*Collecting acorns*

*My pretty shoes*

*What beautiful flowers!*

*Between friends*

# The wolf

# In love

# The koala

# The panda

*Strike a pose!*

*My summer cap*

*The artist at work*

*Colour co-ordinated*

# Three little pigs

# The chef

# The butcher

# The junior chef

*Hot ! Hot ! Hot!*

*Cooking the roast*

*Ready for service*

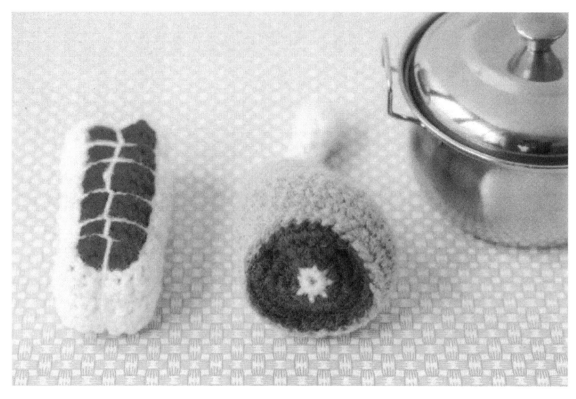

*Today's menu*

# Rabbit's little family

# The mummy bunny and her baby

*The carrot crib*

*Little snack basket*

*Cuddle time*

*Yummy!*

# My animal carry-all

# Patterns

# *Stitches*

## Chain

A chain row is a succession of chain stitches. It is the base for all works crocheted in rows, as well as for some of the works crocheted in rounds or spirals.

## Foundation chain (or base chain)

1. Attach the yarn to the hook with a slip knot. Don't forget to leave enough yarn to thread through at the end.

2. Wrap the yarn over the hook in an anti-clockwise direction from right to left and draw the yarn through the slip knot; this makes a chain stitch that sits under the hook and also a working loop on the hook instead of the slip knot.

3. Wrap the yarn over and draw it through the loop on the hook; this makes another chain stitch that sits under the hook.

4. Repeat step 3 until you have the required number of chain stitches.

To make a chain stitch within a pattern, follow step 3 above.

## Slip stitch

Insert the hook into the chain. Wrap the yarn over the hook and draw it through both the chain and the loop on the hook.

## Double crochet

1. Insert the hook into the chain. Wrap the yarn over the hook and draw it through the chain only: you have two loops on the hook.

2. Wrap the yarn over again and draw it through both loops: you have a double crochet. Only one loop remains on the hook.

***Note*** *A row or a round of double crochets always begins with one chain stitch (unless you work in continuous spirals). It provides the required height; it is not counted as a 'real' stitch. When worked at the end of a row it is called a turning chain.*

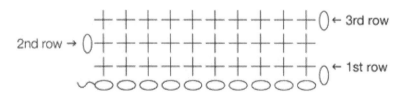

**Stitch diagram for double crochet**

# Half treble

1. Wrap the yarn around the hook then insert the hook into the chain. Wrap the yarn over again and draw it through the chain only: you have three loops on the hook.

2. Wrap the yarn over again and draw it through the three loops on the hook: you have a half treble. There is only the working loop on the hook.

***Note*** *A row or a round of half trebles always begins with two chain stitches They count for one half treble. When working in rows, you crochet the last half treble into the top of the two chain stitches of the previous row. When working in rounds, you join each round with a slip stitch into the top of the two chain stitches of the previous round.*

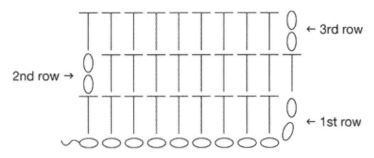

**Stitch diagram for half treble**

## Treble

1. Wrap the yarn around the hook then insert the hook into the chain. Wrap the yarn over again and draw it through the chain: you have three loops on the hook.

2. Wrap the yarn over again and draw it through the first two loops on the hook: you have two loops on the hook.

3. Wrap the yarn over again and draw it through the two loops on the hook: you have a treble.

*Note A row or a round of trebles always begins with three chain stitches They count for one treble. When working in rows, you crochet the last treble into the top of the three chain stitches of the previous row. When working in rounds, you join each round with a slip stitch into the top of the three chain stitches of the previous round.*

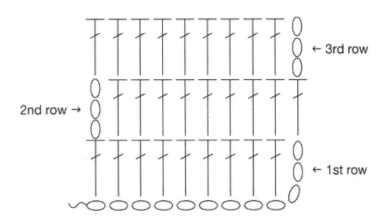

## Stitch diagram for treble

# Abbreviations and symbols

| | |
|---|---|
| beg | Beginning |
| ch | Chain |
| ch-sp | Chain space |
| dc | Double crochet |
| dc2tog | Double crochet 2 together |
| foll | Follow(ing) |
| htr | Half treble |
| htr2tog | Half treble 2 together |
| rep | Repeat |
| RS | Right side |
| sp | Space |
| ss | Slip stitch |
| st | Stitch |
| tog | Together |
| tr | Treble |
| tr2tog | Treble 2 together |
| WS | Wrong side |
| … | Repeat instructions given between asterisks the number of times indicated |

○ ch
+ dc
T tr

**Stitch diagram symbols**

When an instruction is repeated several times within a row or round, it is enclosed by the special symbols *, ° or °°. Perform the instruction, then repeat it the number of times indicated.

**Example:**

*1 dc in the next dc, 2 dc in the next dc*, repeat from *to* twice. (9 dc)

# US and UK crochet terms

## US and UK crochet terms

Be aware that crochet terms in the US are different from those in the UK. This can be confusing as the same terms are used to refer to different stitches under each system. All crochet patterns in this book are written in UK and European terms. US crocheters must take care that they work the correct stitches. One way to tell which system is being used in other patterns is that the American system starts with a single crochet, which the UK system doesn't have; so patterns with 'sc' in them can be identified as American patterns.

| US | UK |
|---|---|
| single crochet (sc) | double crochet (dc) |
| half double crochet (hdc) | half treble (htr) |
| double crochet (dc) | treble (tr) |
| treble (tr) | double treble (dtr) |
| double treble (dtr) | triple treble (tr tr) |
| triple treble (tr tr) | quadruple treble (qtr) |

## Crochet Hook Sizes Conversion Chart

Crochet hooks come in a range of sizes and the size of hook needed is directly related to the thickness of yarn being used. A fine yarn requires a small hook, whilst a thick yarn will need a more chunkier hook. There are two main sizing schemes for crochet hooks: the metric system (used in the UK and Europe) and the American system. The chart here lists the sizes available, with conversions for both systems.

| Metric Sizes | American Sizes |
|---|---|

| | |
|---|---|
| 2.00mm | B1 |
| 2.25mm | B1 |
| 2.50mm | C2 |
| 2.75mm | C2 |
| 3.00mm | D3 |
| 3.25mm | D3 |
| 3.50mm | E4 |
| 3.75mm | F5 |
| 4.00mm | G6 |
| 4.50mm | 7 |
| 5.00mm | H8 |
| 5.50mm | I9 |
| 6.00mm | J10 |
| 6.50mm | K10½ |
| 7.00mm | — |
| 8.00mm | L11 |
| 9.00mm | M/N13 |
| 10.00mm | N/P15 |
| 12.00mm | O16 |
| 15.00mm | P/Q |
| 16.00mm | Q |
| 19.00mm | S |

# Decorations in carded wool

**Carded wool** is wool that has been cleaned and disentangled, but not spun. It is sold in what looks like flat fluffy fibre wisps.

**A felting needle** is a thick spike ending with a thicker part used as a handle. They come in different models that can be ergonomic and with one or more spikes.

You **felt** the carded wool in the crocheted work by tangling the fibres using the felting needle.

## Felting

If the work is not yet filled with toy filling, put a thick, dense, spongy foam pad between the two layers in order not to include the back side of the work while felting.

Put a small amount of carded wool on the crocheted work where it should go and jab it several times. It must fuse with the stitches and look like felted wool. Repeat using small amounts at a time until the whole area is covered as you want. Pay particular attention to the edges so they are neat.

Make a small tight ball of carded wool between your fingers, then jab it with the felting needle so it becomes compact and felted. Wind some more wool around the ball and jab it again. Repeat until you have a ball of the required size. Position it on the crocheted work then jab the needle at the base to fuse it with the stitches.

# *Dimensions*

In this book the materials lists give a good general description of the yarns. You will find on pages a summary of the yarns from Bergère de France that were used to make the photographed models. You are free to choose materials and colours to suit your tastes, projects and the yarns you have available. The same applies to the crochet hook sizes. Yarn can be used with one or two strands with a smaller or larger hook. It all depends on what you want to achieve: density or lightness, softness or rigidity.

Furthermore, no one crochets the same way. Some pull their yarn at each stitch; others let it flow through the fingers. And the tension often changes with the mood! The models in this book do not require precise dimensions so no gauge is indicated. Let yourself fall under the charm of discovery and creativity.

# *Technical notes*

## Working in rows
When working in rows, the stitches are worked from the right towards the left and the work must be turned at the end of each row. It does not matter which way you turn the work, but always turn it the same way. Once the work is turned, remember to place the yarn at the back without wrapping it around the last stitch of the finished row.

## Working in rounds or in a continuous spiral
When working in rounds, the stitches are always worked in the same direction (anti-clockwise) without ever turning the work.

### Working in rounds
Every round is closed by a slip stitch. At the beginning of the round, the hook must be raised to the height of the new stitches by making the required number of chain stitches

### Working in a continuous spiral
The stitches are worked continuously, without closing the round.

## Central ring in chain stitches
Start by working a foundation chain with a few chain stitches. Close it by making a slip stitch into the first chain stitch to form a ring.

For closed pieces (e.g. heads, legs, hat), make the first round by inserting the hook into the centre of the ring. For tubular pieces (e.g. skirt, trouser legs), make the first round by inserting the hook into the stitches themselves.

## Magic ring

Hold the yarn tail in your left hand. Make a loop at least 10cm (4in) away from the beginning of the yarn, with the tail end on the left and the end leading to the ball behind the loop. Insert the hook in the loop through the front, pick up the yarn leading to the ball and draw it back through the loop without closing the main loop. Make 1 chain stitch to secure the loop: you have a working stitch on the hook. Work the first round by inserting the hook into the loop and working over both the loop and the tail end of yarn. At the end of this round, pull on the tail end of the yarn to bring the ring to the requested diameter, or to close it fully.

## Decreasing

To decrease by one stitch, work the following two stitches together. The principle is the same to decrease by any number of stitches.

### Working two double crochets together (dc2tog)

1. Insert the hook through the next stitch. Wrap the yarn over the hook and draw it through the stitch.

2. Insert the hook through the next stitch. Wrap the yarn over and draw the hook through the stitch.

3. Wrap the yarn over the hook and draw it through the three loops now on the hook.

## Working two half trebles together (htr2tog)

1. Wrap the yarn over the hook. Insert the hook through the next stitch. Wrap the yarn over the hook and draw it through the stitch.

2. Wrap the yarn over the hook. Insert the hook through the next stitch. Wrap the yarn over the hook and draw it through the stitch.

3. Wrap the yarn over the hook and draw it through the five loops now on the hook.

## Working two treble togethers (tr2tog)

1. Wrap the yarn over the hook. Insert the hook through the next stitch. Wrap the yarn over the hook and draw it through the stitch. Wrap the yarn over again and draw it through the two loops.

2. Wrap the yarn over the hook. Insert the hook through the next stitch. Wrap the yarn over again and draw the hook through the stitch. Wrap the yarn over again and draw the hook through the first two loops.

3. Wrap the yarn over the hook and draw it through the three loops now on the hook.

## Increasing

Work the requested number of additional stitches into the same stitch.

## Front loop, back loop

At the top of every stitch there are two horizontal bars of yarn: one is the front loop and one is the back loop. When the pattern does not provide any specific instruction, always insert the hook under both loops. Sometimes a pattern tells you to insert the hook through either the front or the back loop of the stitch. In that case follow the instructions carefully to create the requested effect.

*N.B. The front and the back correspond to the two sides of the work as you hold it, not to the right side and wrong side of the work (see below).*

## Right side, wrong side

Crochet stitches look slightly different on one side from how they appear on the other side. In most cases, you can choose which side you prefer. However, for some patterns crocheted in rows, the instructions mention a 'right side' so your end result can match the one shown in the photograph.

## Markers

It is useful to place markers as you work so you don't have to constantly count the number of stitches. It's particularly useful when you work in spirals to mark the beginning of each round. Simply place a piece of yarn between the hook and the working row or round, or use stitch markers (sold in haberdasheries or art and craft shops).

## Joining in a new ball

If possible, join a new ball of yarn at the beginning of a row or round. Cut the old yarn to a minimum of 10cm (4in) from the work and work the first stitch of the new row or round with the new yarn.

## Colour transitions

- If you are in the middle of a row, round or spiral, at the last stitch of the first colour, make the last yarn over with the new yarn.
- At the end of a round, use the new yarn to crochet the slip stitch.

## Threading in another yarn

To thread in another yarn through the work – for example, to crochet an edge – insert the hook through the requested stitch (or row), wrap the yarn over the hook and draw the hook back through the work.

## Fastening off

Cut the yarn to a minimum of 10cm (4in) away from the work. Take the hook off the work and draw the tail end of the yarn through the working stitch. Gently pull the yarn to close the stitch.

## Sewing in the ends

Use a tapestry or darning needle (large eye and blunt point) and the yarn you used to work. When the yarn is difficult to handle (hairy yarn for example), use a thin knitting yarn or a thick embroidery yarn the same colour as your yarn.

Use sewing yarn for buttons and other notions (collar folds, sleeve cuffs etc).

*N.B. The front and the back correspond to the two sides of the work as you hold it, not to the right side and wrong side of the work.*

# Basic elements

*The following instructions are for elements common to several animals. Refer to each pattern for materials, colours and notions as well as for specific instructions.*

## Head

*Applicable for the bear, the raccoon, the koala, the panda and the pigs.*

Make a magic ring. Work in a spiral.
**Round 1** 8 dc into magic ring. Pull yarn to close ring.
**Round 2** 2 dc into each dc to end = 16 dc **Round 3** *1 dc into next dc, 2 dc into foll dc*, rep 7 times from to = 24 dc **Round 4** *1 dc into each of next 2 dc, 2 dc into foll dc*, rep 7 times from to = 32 dc **Round 5** *1 dc into each of next 3 dc, 2 dc into foll dc*, rep 7 times from to = 40 dc **Round 6** *1 dc into each of next 4 dc, 2 dc into foll dc*, rep 7 times from to = 48 dc

**Rounds 7–19** 1 dc into each dc to end **Round 20** *1 dc into each of next 4 dc, dc2tog*, rep 7 times from *to* = 40 dc **Round 21** *1 dc into each of next 3 dc, dc2tog*, rep 7 times from *to* = 32 dc **Round 22** *1 dc into each of next 2 dc, dc2tog*, rep 7 times from *to* = 24 dc Work 1 ss into next dc to finish.
Fasten off.

## Legs and torso
*Applicable for all animals except the wolf and the baby rabbit.*

### Leg 1
Make a magic ring. Work in a spiral.
**Round 1** 12 dc into magic ring. Pull yarn to close ring.
**Rounds 2–30** 1 dc into each dc to end Fasten off.

### Leg 2
Work as for Leg 1, without cutting off the yarn at the end.

### Torso
Work in a spiral.
**Round 1** 4 ch at end of leg 2, 1 dc into each dc of leg 1, 4 ch, 1 dc into each dc of leg 2 = 32 st **Round 2** *1 dc into each of next 4 ch, 1 dc into each of next 12 dc*, rep once from *to* = 32 dc **Rounds 3–18** 1 dc into each dc to end **Round 19** 1 dc into each of next 9 dc, dc2tog, 1 dc into each of foll 14 dc, dc2tog, 1 dc into each of foll 5 dc = 30 dc **Round 20** 1 dc into each of next 9 dc, dc2tog, 1 dc into each of foll 12 dc, dc2tog, 1 dc into each of foll 5 dc = 28 dc **Round 21** 1 dc into each of next 8 dc, dc2tog, 1 dc into each of foll 12 dc, dc2tog, 1 dc into each of foll 4 dc = 26 dc **Round 22** 1 dc into each of next 8 dc, dc2tog, 1 dc into each of foll 10 dc, dc2tog, 1 dc into each of foll 4 dc = 24 dc Work 1 ss into next dc to finish.

Fasten off.

## Arms (x2)

***Applicable for all animals except the wolf and the baby rabbit.***

Make a magic ring. Work in a spiral.

**Round 1** 10 dc into magic ring. Pull yarn to close ring.

**Rounds 2–30** 1 dc into each dc to end Work 1 ss into next dc to finish.

Fasten off.

## Making up

***Applicable for all animals but see also individual patterns.***

Sew in the threads on the WS of the work.

Apply the eyes to the head as per the pattern's instructions.

Fill the head with toy filling.

Close the crotch with 4 small whip stitches.

Fill the torso with toy filling then sew the head on top, stitch by stitch.

Fill the arms with toy filling then sew them to the torso using slip stitches, just under the head.

Add the details specific to each pattern (tail, nose, snout, ears, antlers etc.).

You will find advice for the making up page.

# Shoes

*Almost all shoes in this book are made following one of the three styles below. Refer to each pattern for specific material, colours and details.*

## Flat shoes (x2)

Make 9 ch. Work in rows.
**Row 1** (RS) 1 dc into 2nd ch from hook, 1 dc into each foll ch to end = 8 dc **Rows 2–5** 1 ch, 1 dc into each dc to end Continue in a spiral.
**Round 1** On short side of work, 1 dc into each of rows 4–1; on foundation chain, skip 1 ch, 1 dc into each of next 7 ch; on other short side, 1 dc into each of rows 1–4; on row 5, skip 1 dc, 1 dc into each of next 7 dc = 22 dc **Round 2** 1 dc into back loop of each dc to end **Round 3** dc2tog twice, 1 dc into each of next 17 dc (there is 1 dc left on that round) **Round 4** dc2tog twice, 1 dc into each of next 15 dc (there is 1 dc left on that round) **Round 5** dc2tog twice, 1 dc into each of next 14 dc = 16 st Fasten off.
Sew in the threads on the WS.

## Cuffed shoes (x2)

Work as per low shoes, to end of round 5 = 16 dc.
Turn. Continue in rows.
**Rows 1–4** 1 ch, 1 dc into each dc to end Fasten off.
Sew in the threads on the WS.

*Safety*

**If the animals are for very young children,** a few safety procedures are essential. Only use smooth yarns (no hairy yarns) and filling described as safety toy filling. Replace plastic eyes with embroidery stitches. Carefully sew in all the threads on the inside. Avoid all decorations that could be ripped away and swallowed (beads, safety pins, etc).

# Boots (x2)

Work as per low shoes, to end of round 5 = 16 dc.

**Rounds 6–12** 1 dc into each dc to end Work 1 ss into next dc to finish.

Fasten off.

Sew in the threads on the WS.

# Armatures

*If your animals are made strictly for decorative purposes and won't be used as toys, you can add an internal wire framework, or armature, so they can be articulated.*

Use 3mm (⅛in) aluminium wire. Work it with jewellery-making tools: a wire cutter and flat-nose pliers. Cut two wires of about 40cm (16in) and two more of about 25cm (9¾in). On each, make a small loop at one end. After the first round of the torso, insert the longest wires in the legs with the loop pointing downwards. Continue to crochet the torso around the wires so that they go out through the neck after the last round of the torso.

When filling the torso with toy filling, ensure the wires are placed at equal distance of the work. Stick the wires in the head filled with toy filling.

Insert the remaining wires in the arms, with the small loop pointing downwards. Fill in the arms, making sure the armatures remain in the centre of the arm. Stick the wires sideways in the torso and the head.

Photos on pages 14 to 17

# *The bear*

## Materials for the bear
- Yarn 40% combed wool, 40% acrylic and 20% mohair for crochet hook 4mm: 2 skeins light brown
- Carded wool, black
- 2 solid eyes with shank backs, black, size 10mm (⅜in)
- Toy filling
- Crochet hook 4mm
- Scissors
- Wool needle
- Felting needle

## Head, legs, torso and arms

Work as indicated on page.

## Nose

Work as for head, to end of round 4 = 32 dc.
**Rounds 5–8** 1 dc into each dc to end
Work 1 ss into next dc to finish.
Fasten off.

## Ears (x2)

Work as for head, to end of round 2 = 16 dc.
**Rounds 3–8** 1 dc into each dc to end
Work 1 ss into next dc to finish.
Fasten off.

## Making up

Work as indicated on page. Fix the eyes on round 11 of the head, spacing them out by 12 dc.

Fill in nose with toy filling then sew it under the eyes.
Use carded wool and felting needle to make an oval horizontal nose prolonged by a vertical line downwards (see instructions page. Sew on ears, pinching them at base.

## Materials for walking kit

- Yarn 100% acrylic for crochet hook 3.5mm: 1 skein light green (yarn A), 1 skein dark green (yarn B), 1 skein brown (yarn C), 1 skein light brown (yarn D)
- 2 snap fasteners 10mm (½in)
- Lacing tape, leather (or vinyl, felt etc.) 55cm (21.5in) long 10mm (½in) wide

- Spare cardboard piece for making the pompom
- Sewing thread
- Crochet hook 4mm
- Tapestry needle
- Sewing kit

# Jumper

## Main piece
With yarn A make 41 ch. Work in rows.
**Row 1** (RS) 1 dc into 2nd from hook, 1 dc in each ch to end = 40 dc
**Rows 2–12** 1 ch, 1 dc into each dc to end **Row 13** With yarn B, 1 ch, 1 dc into each dc to end **Rows 14–15** With yarn A, as row 13
**Row 16** With yarn B, as row 13

## Left back
**Row 17** With yarn A, 1 ch, 1 dc into each of next 9 dc, turn **Rows 18–24** As row 13, working only on 9 dc Fasten off.

## Front
On RS, re-join yarn A in 11th dc of row 16.
**Row 17** 1 ch, 1 dc into dc where yarn was re-joined, 1 dc into each of next 19 dc, turn **Rows 18–24** As row 13, working only on central 20 dc Fasten off.

## Right back
On RS, re-join yarn A in 32nd dc of row 16.
**Row 17** 1 ch, 1 dc into dc where yarn was re-joined, 1 dc into each rem dc **Rows 18–24** As row 13, working only on 9 dc Fasten off.

## Turtleneck collar
On RS, re-join yarn B in 1st dc of left back.

**Row 25** 1 ch, 1 dc into each of 9 dc of left back, 1 ch, 1 dc into each of 20 dc of front, 1 ch, 1 dc into each of 9 dc of right back = 40 st **Row 26** 1 ch, 1 dc into each st to end = 40 dc **Rows 27–40** 1 ch, 1 dc into each dc to end Fasten off.

## Sleeves

### Right sleeve

On RS, re-join yarn A in free dc at base of right armhole. Work in a spiral.
**Round 1** 1 ch, 1 dc into dc where yarn A was re-joined, 1 dc into each of rows 17–24 of right back, 1 dc into ch at top of armhole, 1 dc into each of rows 24–17 of front = 18 dc **Rounds 2–22** 1 dc into each dc to end Turn (so the cuff is on the RS once folded).
Continue with yarn B.
**Round 23** 2 dc into 1st dc, 1 dc into foll dc to end = 19 dc **Rounds 24–30** 1 dc into each dc to end
Work 1 ss into next dc to finish.
Fasten off.

### Left sleeve

Work as for right sleeve (in round 1, work into each of rows 17–24 of front, then into each of rows 24–17 of left back).

### Finishing

Sew in threads on WS. Sew snap fasteners on two backs, on rows 4 and 13. Fold turtleneck 3 times outwards. At each end of turtleneck, thread a long tail of yarn B through the three layers and knot the two tails together. Knot the four tails together with a bow to close the collar.
Turn the sleeve cuffs.

## Shorts

Work with yarn B.

Work with yarn B.

### Left leg
Make 20 ch, join with a ss to form ring. Work in a spiral.

**Round 1** 1 ch, 1 dc into same ch, 1 dc into each foll ch to end = 20 dc

**Rounds 2–10** 1 dc into each dc to end

Fasten off.

### Right leg
Work as for left leg, without cutting the yarn at the end.

### Top part
Work in a spiral.

**Round 1** 2 ch at end of right leg, 1 dc into each dc of left leg, 2 ch, 1 dc into each dc of right leg = 44 st **Round 2** *1 dc into each of next 2 ch, 1 dc into each of foll 20 dc*, rep once from to = 44 dc **Rounds 3–18** 1 dc into each dc to end

Work 1 ss into next dc to arrive at middle of back. Turn. Continue in rows.

**Rows 1–6** 1 ch, 1 dc into each of 44 dc

**Row 7** 3 ch (=1 tr), skip 1 dc at base of 3 ch, 1 tr into each of next dc = 44 tr Fasten off.

### Finishing
Sew in threads on WS. Close crotch with 2 small whip stitches. With yarn B make 70 ch then sew in the tails on WS. Weave foundation chain between tr of the last row. Fold 5 rounds outwards at legs' hem.

## Hat
With yarn A, make a magic ring.

Work in a spiral.

**Rounds 1–6** Work as for head = 48 dc

**Round 7** *6 ch, skip 6 dc, 1 dc into each of foll 5 dc, 2 dc into next dc, 1 dc into each of foll 6 dc, 2 dc into next dc, 1 dc into each of foll 5 dc*, rep once from *to* = 52 st **Round 8** 1 dc into each st to end = 52 dc **Rounds 9–17** 1 dc into each dc to end

**Round 18** 1 ss into next dc, 3 ch (=1 tr, 1 tr into each of foll dc, 1 ss at top of 3 ch = 52 tr Fasten off.

## Finishing
Sew in threads on WS. With yarn B make a 4cm (1½in pompom and sew it on top of hat. Fold round of tr outwards.

## Heeled shoes
With yarn C, work as indicated on page.

## Backpack
Work with yarn D.

### Bottom
Make 16 ch. Work in rows.
**Row 1** (RS 1 dc into 2nd ch from hook, 1 dc into each foll ch to end = 15 dc **Rows 2–7** 1 ch, 1 dc into each dc to end

### Walls
Continue in a spiral.
**Round 1** Turn on side, 1 dc into each of rows 6–1, 1 dc into each of first 15 ch of foundation chain, 1 dc into each of rows 1–6, 1 dc into each of 15 dc of row 7 = 42 dc **Round 2** 1 dc into back loop of each dc to end **Rounds 3–20** 1 dc into each dc to end

### Flap
Turn. Continue in rows.

**Row 1** 1 ch, 1 dc into each of first 15 dc, turn **Rows 2–8** 1 ch, 1 dc into each dc to end
**Row 9** dc2tog, 1 dc into each next dc to end = 14 dc **Rows 10–14** As row 9 = 9 dc
Fasten off.

## Pockets (x2)
Make 11 ch. Work in rows.
**Row 1** 1 dc into 2nd ch from hook, 1 dc into each foll ch to end = 10 dc
**Rows 2–12** 1 ch, 1 dc into each dc to end Fasten off.

### Finishing
Sew in threads on WS. Sew pockets onto main piece using whip stitches: align pockets with round 2 of the wall; towards back, align them with fold; towards front, sew them slightly diagonally to allow some widening at opening.

Cut two 70cm (27½in) pieces of yarn C and fold in half. Fix one at base of right side of the flap, weave it in between all dc of last row of wall and thread it through middle of front. Rep with other piece of yarn C working from base of left side of flap towards middle of front.

Cut two laces of 25cm (9¾in) each. Insert one end of both laces in middle of row 1 of flap, fold it and fix with a few stitches. Sew other end of each lace at base of each pocket.

Cut last piece of lacing tape to a width of 1cm (⅜in) and cut one end in an arrow shape. Fix other end to centre of fold, on row 12, using a cross stitch.

Photos on pages 18 to 21

# *The raccoon*

## Materials for the raccoon

- Yarn 100% acrylic for crochet hook 3.5mm: 2 skeins light grey (yarn A), 1 skein black (yarn B), 1 skein white (yarn C)
- Carded wool, black
- 2 solid eyes with shank backs, white, size 15mm
- Toy filling
- Crochet hook 4mm
- Scissors
- Wool needle
- Felting needle

## Head, legs, torso and arms

Work with yarn A, as indicated on page

## Tail

Make a magic ring with yarn B.

Work in a spiral.

**Round 1** 6 dc into magic ring. Pull yarn to close ring.

**Round 2** *1 dc into each of next 2 dc, 2 dc into foll dc*, rep once from *to* = 8 dc **Round 3** *1 dc into each of next 3 dc, 2 dc into foll dc*, rep once from *to* = 10 dc **Round 4** *1 dc into each of next 4 dc, 2 dc into foll dc*, rep once from *to* = 12 dc **Round 5** *1 dc into each of next 5 dc, 2 dc into foll dc*, rep once from *to* = 14 dc **Round 6** *1 dc into each of next 6 dc, 2 dc into foll dc*, rep once from *to* = 16 dc **Round 7** *1 dc into each of next 7 dc, 2 dc into foll dc*, rep once from *to* = 18 dc **Round 8** *1 dc into each of next 8 dc, 2 dc into foll dc*, rep once from *to* = 20 dc **Round 9** *1 dc into each of the 9 dc, 2 dc into foll dc*, rep once from *to* = 22 dc **Round 10** *1 dc into each of next 10 dc, 2 dc into foll dc*, rep once from *to* = 24 dc **Round 11** *1 dc into each of next 11 dc, 2 dc into foll dc*, rep once from *to* = 26 dc **Rounds 12–13** With yarn B, 1 dc into each dc to end **Rounds 14–16** With yarn A, 1 dc into each dc to end **Rounds 17–19** As for rounds 12–13

**Round 20** With yarn A, dc2tog, 1 dc into each foll dc to end = 25 dc

**Rounds 21–22** With yarn A, as round 20 = 23 dc

**Rounds 23–25** With yarn B, as round 20 = 20 dc

**Rounds 26–28** With yarn A, as round 20 = 17 dc

**Rounds 29–31** With yarn B, as round 20 = 14 dc

Fill the work with toy filling.

**Rounds 32–37** Rep once rounds 26–31 = 8 dc

**Round 38** With yarn A, as round 20 = 7 dc

**Rounds 39–40** With yarn A, 1 dc into each dc to end Work 1 ss into next dc to finish.

Fasten off.

## Nose

With yarn C work as for head, to end of round 2 = 16 dc.
**Round 3** *1 dc into each of next 7 dc, 2 dc into foll dc*, rep once from *to* = 18 dc **Rounds 4–6** 1 dc into each dc to end
Work 1 ss into next dc to finish.
Fasten off.

## Ears (x 2)

With yarn A, work as for tail, to end of round 7 = 18 dc.
**Rounds 8–9** 1 dc into each dc to end
Take the hook off the working loop and enlarge the loop or place it onto a stitch marker so the work doesn't become undone during the next stage.
Using the felting needle, apply the carded wool on one side of the ear (see instructions page).
Put the working loop back on the hook.
Close the base of the ear by crocheting 1 row of dc through the two layers = 9 dc.
Fasten off.

## Making up

Work as indicated on page. Before fixing the eyes, create a mask with the carded wool to go all around the head, using the felting needle: place it between rounds 10 and 16 of the front and thin it at the back (see instructions page .

Fix the eyes on the mask, spacing them by 14 dc.

Fill in the nose with toy filling then sew it under the mask.

With the carded wool make a small oval horizontal nose, prolonged by a vertical line.

Sew the ears to the head. Sew the tail to the back of the raccoon, 4 rounds above the crotch.

## Materials for striped clothing

- Yarn 60% acrylic, 20% combed wool and 20% polyamide for crochet hook 3.00mm: 1 skein medium grey (yarn A)
- Yarn 100% acrylic for crochet hook 3.5mm: 1 skein dark grey (yarn B), 1 skein red (yarn C)
- Carded wool, black
- 3 snap fasteners 10mm (0.4in)
- Sewing thread
- Crochet hook 4mm
- Wool needle
- Sewing kit

## Overall

### Main piece

**Left leg**
With yarn B, make 18 ch, join with a ss to form ring. Work in a spiral.
**Round 1** 1 ch (not counted as a st), 1 dc into same ch, 1 dc into each foll ch to end = 18 dc **Rounds 2–24** 1 dc into each dc, alternating yarns A and B every 2 rounds (ending with 2 rounds in yarn A). Fasten off.

**Right leg**
Work as for left leg, without cutting the yarn at the end.

**Body**
Work in a spiral.

**Round 1** With yarn B, 4 ch at end of right leg, 1 dc into each dc of left leg, 4 ch, 1 dc into each dc of right leg = 44 st **Round 2** With yarn B, *1 dc into each of next 4 ch, 1 dc into each of foll 18 dc*, rep once from *to* = 44 dc **Rounds 3–4** With yarn A, 1 dc into each dc to end

**Round 5** With yarn B, 1 dc into each dc to end

With yarn B, 1 dc into each of foll 2 dc (to arrive at the middle of the back).

Turn. Continue in rows.

**Row 1** (RS) With yarn B, 1 ch, 1 dc into each dc to end **Rows 2–3** With yarn A, as row 1

**Rows 4–5** With yarn B, as row 1

**Rows 6–19** Rep 3 times rows 2–5, then rep once rows 2–3 (ending with 2 rows in yarn A)

**Left back**

**Row 20** With yarn B, 1 ch, 1 dc into each of first 10 dc, turn **Row 21** With yarn B, 1 ch, 1 dc into each of next 10 dc **Rows 22–23** With yarn A, as row 21

**Rows 24–25** With yarn B, as row 21

Fasten off.

**Front**

On the RS, re-join yarn B in 13th dc of row 19.

**Row 20** 1 ch, 1 dc into dc where yarn was re-joined, 1 dc into each of next 19 dc, turn **Row 21** 1 ch, 1 dc into each of next 20 dc

**Rows 22–23** With yarn A, as row 21

**Rows 24–25** With yarn B, as row 21

Fasten off.

**Right back**

On the RS, re-join yarn B in 35th dc of row 19.

**Row 20** 1 ch, 1 dc into dc where yarn was re-joined, 1 dc into each of next 9 dc **Row 21** 1 ch, 1 dc into each of next 10 dc
**Rows 22–23** With yarn A, as row 21
**Rows 24–25** With yarn B, as row 21

### Neckline
**Row 26** With yarn A, 1 ch, 1 dc into each of 10 dc from right back, 1 dc into each of 20 dc from front, 1 dc into each of 10 dc from left back = 40 dc Fasten off.

## Sleeves

### Right sleeve
On the RS, re-join yarn B in 1st free dc at base of right armhole. Work in a spiral.
**Round 1** 1 ch, 1 dc into dc where yarn was re-joined, 1 dc into free dc, 1 dc into each of 6 rows from right back, 1 dc into each of 6 rows from front = 14 dc **Round 2** 1 dc into each dc to end
**Rounds 3–4** With yarn A, as round 2
**Rounds 5–6** With yarn B, as round 2
**Rounds 7–26** Rep 5 times rounds 3–6 (ending with 2 rounds in yarn B). Work 1 ss into next dc to finish.
Fasten off.

### Left sleeve
Work as for right sleeve (for round 1, work on the rows from the front then from the left back).

## Finishing
Sew in the threads on the WS. Close the crotch with 4 small whip stitches. Sew the snap fasteners on the two sides of the back on rounds 9, 17 and 25.

# Kerchief

With yarn C in double, make 2 ch. Work in rows.

**Row 1** 1 dc into 2nd ch from hook, 1 dc into next ch = 2 dc **Row 2** 1 ch, 2 dc into each dc = 4 dc

**Row 3** 1 ch, 2 dc into 1st dc, 1 dc into each foll dc to last dc, 2 dc into last dc = 6 dc **Rows 4–14** As row 3 = 28 dc

## Lace and edge

With yarn C, make 20 ch, work 24 dc evenly along one slanted edge of the kerchief, 3 dc in the pointed end, 24 dc evenly along the other slanted edge, 20 ch.

Fasten off.

Sew in the threads on the WS.

Photos on pages 22 to 23 and 27

# *The fox*

## Materials for the fox

- Yarn 100% acrylic for crochet hook 3.5mm: 2 skeins orange (yarn A), 1 skein off white (yarn B), 1 skein black (yarn C)
- 2 solid eyes with shank backs, colour white, size 15mm (⅝in)
- Toy filling
- Crochet hook 4mm
- Scissors
- Wool needle
- Felting needle

## Head

With yarn C, make a magic ring.
Work in a spiral.

**Round 1** 8 dc into magic ring. Pull yarn to close ring.

**Rounds 2–3** 1 dc into each dc

**Round 4** *1 dc into each of next 3 dc, 2 dc into foll dc*, rep once from *to* = 10 dc **Round 5** *1 dc into each of next 4 dc, 2 dc into foll dc*, rep once from *to* = 12 dc **Round 6** *1 dc into each of next 5 dc, 2 dc into foll dc*, rep once from *to* = 14 dc **Round 7** *1 dc into each of next 6 dc, 2 dc into foll dc*, rep once from *to* = 16 dc **Round 8** *1 dc into each of next 7 dc, 2 dc into foll dc*, rep once from *to* = 18 dc **Round 9** *1 dc into each of next 8 dc, 2 dc into foll dc*, rep once from *to* = 20 dc **Round 10** *1 dc into each of next 9 dc, 2 dc into foll dc*, rep once from *to* = 22 dc **Round 11** *1 dc into each of next 10 dc, 2 dc into foll dc*, rep once from *to* = 24 dc **Round 12** *1 dc into each of next 11 dc, 2 dc into foll dc*, rep once from *to* = 26 dc **Round 13** *1 dc into each of next 12 dc, 2 dc into foll dc*, rep once from *to* = 28 dc **Round 14** *1 dc into each of next 13 dc, 2 dc into foll dc*, rep once from *to* = 30 dc **Round 15** *1 dc into each of next 14 dc, 2 dc into foll dc*, rep once from *to* = 32 dc **Round 16** *1 dc into next dc, 2 dc into foll dc*, rep 15 times from *to* = 48 dc **Rounds 17–28** 1 dc into each dc to end

Fix the eyes on round 15, spacing them out by 12 dc.

Fill in the work with toy filling and keep filling as you crochet the next rounds.

**Round 29** *1 dc into each of next 4 dc, dc2tog*, rep 7 times from *to* = 40 dc

**Round 30** *1 dc into each of next 3 dc, dc2tog*, rep 7 times from *to* = 32 dc

**Round 31** *1 dc into each of next 2 dc, dc2tog*, rep 7 times from *to* = 24 dc

**Round 32** *1 dc into each next dc, dc2tog*, rep 7 times from *to* = 16 dc

**Round 33** dc2tog to end = 8 dc

**Round 34** dc2tog to end = 4 dc

Cut the yarn. Thread it through all dc of last round, pull on yarn to close the head then fasten off.

# Legs, torso and arms

With yarn A, work as indicated on page.

## Tail

Work as for raccoon's tail, page. Make a magic ring and work first 10 rounds with yarn B, then continue to end with yarn A.

## Ears (x 2)

With yarn A, work as for tail to end of round 7 = 18 dc.
**Rounds 8–9** 1 dc into each dc to end
Close the base of the ear by crocheting 1 row of ss through the two layers = 9 ss.
Fasten off.

## Making up

Work as indicated on page.
Sew the tail on the back of the fox, 4 rounds above the crotch.

## Materials for Sunday clothes

- Yarn 100% acrylic for crochet hook 3.5mm: 2 skeins yellow (yarn A), 1 skein white (yarn B), 1 skein brown (C)
- 40cm x 5cm (15.75in x 2in) pink felt
- 2 snap fasteners 10mm (0.4in)
- 1 button 10mm (0.4in)
- Sewing thread
- Crochet hook 4mm
- Wool needle
- Sewing kit

## Vest

## Body

With yarn A, make 43 ch. Work in rows.
**Row 1** (RS) 1 dc into 2nd ch from hook, 1 dc into each of foll dc to end = 42 dc **Row 2** 1 ch, 1 dc into each dc to end
**Rows 3–14** As row 2

### Right front

**Row 15** 1 ch, 1 dc into each of next 10 dc, turn **Rows 16–20** As row 2, working only on 10 st
**Row 21** 1 ss into each of next 3 dc, 1 ch, 1 dc into each of foll 7 dc = 7 dc
**Row 22** 1 ch, 1 dc into each dc to end
Fasten off.

### Back

On RS, re-join yarn A in 12th dc from row 14.
**Row 15** 1 ch, 1 dc into dc where yarn was re-joined, 1 dc in each of foll 19 dc, turn **Rows 16–22** As row 2, working only on central 20 st Fasten off.

### Left front

On RS, re-join yarn A in 33rd dc from row 14.
**Row 15** 1 ch, 1 dc into dc where yarn was re-joined, 1 dc in each of foll 9 dc **Rows 16–20** As row 2, working only on 10 st
**Row 21** 1 ch, 1 dc into each of foll 7 dc, turn **Row 22** 1 ch, 1 dc into each dc to end
Fasten off.

## Sleeves

Sew the fronts and back together along 3 dc (armhole-side) to form the shoulders.

### Right sleeve

### Right sleeve

On RS, re-join yarn A in free dc at base of right armhole. Work in a spiral.
**Round 1** 1 ch, 1 dc into the dc where yarn was re-joined, 1 dc into each of rows 15–22 of back, 1 dc into shoulder seam, 1 dc into each of rows 22–15 of right front = 18 dc **Rounds 2–30** 1 dc into each dc to end
Work 1 ss into next dc to finish.
Fasten off.

### Left sleeve

Work as for right sleeve (at round 1, work on rows 15–22 of left front then rows 22–15 of back).

### Back collar

With yarn B, make 29 ch. Work in rows.
**Row 1** 1 dc into 2nd ch from hook, 1 dc into each of next ch to end = 28 dc **Rows 2–4** 1 ch, 1 dc into each dc to end
Fasten off.

### Pockets (x 2

With yarn A, make 7 ch.
**Row 1** 1 dc into 2nd ch from hook, 1 dc into each of next dc to end = 6 dc
**Rows 2–6** 1 ch, 1 dc into each dc to end
Fasten off.

### Finishing

Sew in the threads on WS. To shape the collar, fold the two extremities onto the front and fix them with small stitches. Sew the back collar on the WS of the vest, centred on the back. Sew the pockets on the fronts, horizontally aligned on each side and 2 rows from the bottom edge. Sew the snap fasteners on the fronts, on row 3 and at the base of the collar.

## Trousers

Work with yarn A.

### Left leg
Make 18 ch and join with a ss to form a ring.
Work in a spiral.
**Round 1** 1 ch, 1 dc into same ch, 1 dc into each foll ch to end = 18 dc
**Rounds 2–19** 1 dc into each dc to end
Fasten off.

### Right leg
Work as for left leg, without cutting the yarn at the end.

### Top part
Work in a spiral.
**Round 1** 4 ch at end of right leg, 1 dc into each dc of left leg, 4 ch, 1 dc into each dc of right leg = 44 st **Round 2** *1 dc into each of next 4 ch, 1 dc into each of foll 18 dc*, rep once from *to* = 44 dc **Rounds 3–4** 1 dc into each dc to end
1 dc into each of next 2 dc (to arrive at centre of back). Turn. Continue in rows.
**Rows 1–6** 1 ch, 1 dc into each dc to end = 44 dc At end of row 6, make 5 ch.
Fasten off.

### Finishing
Sew in the threads on WS. Close the crotch with 4 small whip stitches. Fold the free 5 ch onto themselves and sew to make a button loop. Sew the button on the opposite side.

## Tie
Cut the felt in the shape of a tie by thinning it symmetrically along its

length and cutting the corners of each end to make them pointy. Tie it around fox's neck.

## Heeled shoes
With yarn C, work as indicated on page.

Photos on pages 24 to 27

# *The deer*

## Materials for the deer

- Yarn 40% combed wool, 40% acrylic and 20% mohair for crochet hook 4mm: 2 skeins light khaki (yarn A), 1 skein dark khaki (yarn B), 1 skein beige (yarn C)
- Carded wool, black
- 2 solid eyes with shank backs, matt black, size 15mm (⅝in)
- Toy filling
- Crochet hook 4mm
- Scissors
- Wool needle
- Felting needle

## Head

## Head

With yarn A, work as indicated on page to end of row 4 = 32 dc. **Round 5** *1 dc into each of next 4 dc, 2 dc into foll dc*, rep 5 times from *to* , 1 dc in each of last 2 dc = 38 dc **Rounds 6–15** 1 dc into each dc to end **Round 16** *1 dc into each of next 7 dc, dc2tog*, rep 3 times from *to* , 1 dc into each of last 2 dc = 34 dc **Round 17** *1 dc into each of next 6 dc, dc2tog*, rep 3 times from *to* , 1 dc into each of last 2 dc = 30 dc **Round 18** *1 dc into each of next 5 dc, dc2tog*, rep 3 times from *to* , 1 dc into each of last 2 dc = 26 dc Continue with yarn B.

**Round 19** *1 dc into each of next 4 dc, dc2tog*, rep 3 times from *to* , 1 dc into each of last 2 dc = 22 dc **Round 20** *1 dc into each of next 3 dc, dc2tog*, rep 3 times from *to* , 1 dc into each of last 2 dc = 18 dc Fix the eyes at the base of the part worked in yarn B, spacing them out by 8 dc. Fill with toy filling and continue to do so as you work the foll rounds.

**Round 21** *1 dc into each of next 2 dc, dc2tog*, rep 3 times from *to* , 1 dc into each of last 2 dc = 14 dc **Round 22** *1 dc into next dc, dc2tog*, rep 3 times from *to* , 1 dc into each of last 2 dc = 10 dc **Round 23** *dc2tog*, rep 4 times from *to* = 5 dc Thread the yarn into all dc of the last round, pull on the yarn to close the head then fasten off.

## Legs, torso and arms

With yarn A, work as indicated on page.

## Nose

With yarn A, make a magic ring. Work in a spiral.

**Round 1** 8 dc into magic ring. Pull yarn to close ring.

**Round 2** 2 dc into each dc = 16 dc

**Round 3** *1 dc into next dc, 2 dc into foll dc* , rep 7 times from *to* = 24 dc

**Round 4** *1 dc into each of next 2 dc, 2 dc into foll dc*, rep 7 times from *to*

= 32 dc **Round 5** *1 dc into each of next 15 dc, 2 dc into foll dc* , rep once from *to* = 34 dc **Rounds 6–10** 1 dc into each dc to end

Work 1 ss into next dc to finish.

Fasten off.

# Ears (x 2)

With yarn B, make a magic ring. Work in a spiral.

**Round 1** 6 dc into magic ring. Pull yarn to close ring.

**Round 2** *1 dc into each of next 2 dc, 2 dc into foll dc* , rep once from *to* = 8 dc **Round 3** *1 dc into each of next 3 dc, 2 dc into foll dc* , rep once from *to* = 10 dc **Rounds 4–10** 1 dc into each dc to end

Close the base of the ears by working 1 row of ss through the two layers = 5 ss.

Fasten off.

# Antlers (x 2)

With yarn C, make 13 ch.

Work in a spiral.

**Round 1** 1 dc into 2nd ch from hook, 1 dc into each of next 10 ch, 3 dc into last ch; on other side of foundation chain, 1 dc into each of next 10 ch, 2 dc into last ch = 26 dc **Round 2** *1 dc into each of next 12 dc, 2 dc into foll dc*, rep once from *to* = 28 dc **Round 3** *1 dc into each of next 13 dc, 2 dc into foll dc*, rep once from *to* = 30 dc **Round 4** *1 dc into each of next 14 dc, 2 dc into foll dc*, rep once from *to* = 32 dc **Round 5** *1 dc into each of next 15 dc, 2 dc into foll dc*, rep once from *to* = 34 dc **Round 6** 1 dc into each of next 5 dc, *6 ch, 1 dc into 2nd ch from the hook, 1 dc into each of the next 4 ch, 1 dc into each of foll 3 dc*, rep 8 times from *to* , 1 dc into each of the last 2 dc = 9 picots Fold the work in two. Work 1 ss into each of the first 3 dc, working through the two layers.

Fasten off.

## Making up

Work as indicated on page. Fill nose with toy filling, then sew it with slip stitches, aligning it with the point where yarn B begins. With carded wool and felting needle, make two round nostrils positioning them on the nose as shown in the photo above. Sew on ears, then sew antlers above them.

## Materials for clothing

- Yarn 40% combed wool, 30% acrylic and 30% polyamide for crochet hook 3.5mm: 1 skein blue (yarn A)
- Yarn 100% acrylic for crochet hook 3.5mm: 1 skein white (yarn B), 1 skein brown (yarn C), 1 skein light brown (yarn D)
- 3 snap fasteners 10mm (⅜in)
- Sewing thread
- Crochet hook 4mm
- Wool needle
- Sewing kit

## Jumper

### Body
With yarn A, make 35 ch. Work in rows.
**Row 1** (RS) 1 dc into 2nd ch from hook, 1 dc into each foll ch to end = 34 dc **Row 2** 1 ch, 1 dc into each dc to end
**Rows 3–20** As row 2

### Left back
**Row 21** 1 ch, 1 dc into each of the foll 9 dc, turn **Rows 22–28** As row 2, working only on 9 dc
Fasten off.

## Front

On RS, re-join yarn A into 11th dc from row 20.

**Row 21** 1 ch, 1 dc into the dc where yarn was re-joined, 1 dc into each of foll 13 dc, turn **Rows 22–26** As row 2, working only on central 14 dc **Row 27** dc2tog, 1 dc into each foll dc = 13 dc

**Row 28** As row 27 = 12 dc

Fasten off.

## Right back

On RS, re-join yarn A in 26th dc from row 20.

**Row 21** 1 ch, 1 dc into the dc where yarn was re-joined, 1 dc into each of foll 8 dc **Rows 22–28** As row 2, working only on 9 dc

Fasten off.

## Collar

### Left side

On RS, re-join yarn B in 1st dc of left back.

**Row 1** 1 ch, 1 dc into each of 9 dc from left back, 1 dc into each of first 6 dc of front, turn = 15 dc **Rows 2–6** 1 ch, 1 dc into each dc to end

Cut yarn and fasten off.

### Right side

On RS, re-join yarn B to dc immediately after left side of collar.

Work as for left side, work 6 rows of dc.

Fasten off.

## Sleeves

### Right sleeve

On RS, re-join yarn A in free dc at the base of right armhole. Work in a spiral.

**Round 1** 1 ch, 1 dc into dc where yarn was re-joined, 1 dc into rows 21–28 of right back, 1 dc into rows 28–21 of front = 17 dc **Rounds 2–22** 1 dc into each dc to end

Work 1 ss into next dc to finish.

Fasten off.

### Left sleeve
Work as for right sleeve (on round 1, work first through rows 21–28 of front then through rows 28–21 of left back)

### Finishing
Sew in threads on WS. Fold collar onto body of jumper. At each end of collar, thread a long tail of yarn B through both layers and tie the two tails together.

Tie the four tails together with a bow to close the collar.

Sew snap fasteners on back sides: one at base of collar, one on row 2, and last one between two already sewn.

## Golf trousers
Work with yarn C.

### Left leg
Make 22 ch and join with a ss to form a ring.

Work in a spiral.

**Round 1** 1 ch, 1 dc in each dc to end = 22 dc

**Rounds 2–3** 1 dc into each dc to end

**Round 4** *1 dc into each of next 10 dc, dc2tog, rep once from to* = 21 dc

**Round 5** dc2tog, 1 dc into each of foll 19 dc = 20 dc **Round 6** *1 dc into each of next 9 dc, dc2tog, rep once from to* = 19 dc **Round 7** dc2tog, 1 dc into each of next foll 17 dc = 18 dc **Rounds 8–18** 1 dc into each dc to end

Fasten off.

### Right leg
Work as for left leg, without cutting the yarn at the end.

### Top part
Work in a spiral.

**Round 1** 4 ch at end of right leg, 1 dc into each dc of left leg, 4 ch, 1 dc into each dc of right leg = 44 dc **Round 2** *1 dc into each of next 4 ch, 1 dc into each of foll 18 dc*, rep once from *to* = 44 dc **Rounds 3–4** 1 dc into each dc to end

**1 dc** into each of next 2 dc (to arrive at centre of back. Turn. Continue in rows.

**Rows 1–6** 1 ch, 1 dc into each of the foll 44 dc At end of row 6, make 25 ch.

Fasten off.

Re-join yarn C in 1st dc of row 6, make 25 ch, cut the yarn and fasten off. Sew in threads in WS. Close the crotch with 4 small whip stitches. Tie the two lengths of chain stitches together to close the trousers

## Heeled shoes
With yarn D, work as indicated on page.

Work 1 round of dc around the sole by inserting the hook under the free loop of the dc of round 2.

Photos on pages 28 to 29

# *The wolf*

## Materials for the wolf

- Hairy yarn 100% polyamide for crochet hook 9mm: 2 skeins medium grey (yarn A)
- Yarn 100% acrylic for crochet hook 3.5mm: 1 skein dark grey (yarn B)
- Carded wool, black
- 1 grey zip 22cm (8½in) long
- 2 solid eyes with shank backs, light green, size 20mm (¾in)
- Toy filling
- Crochet hook 6mm
- Wool needle
- Felting needle
- Sewing kit

# Head

With yarn A, make a magic ring. Work in a spiral.

**Round 1** 8 dc into magic ring. Pull yarn to close ring.

**Round 2** *1 dc into each of next 3 dc, 2 dc into foll dc*, rep once from *to* = 10 dc **Round 3** *1 dc into each of next 4 dc, 2 dc into foll dc*, rep once from *to* = 12 dc **Round 4** *1 dc into each of next 5 dc, 2 dc into foll dc*, rep once from *to* = 14 dc **Round 5** *1 dc into each of next 6 dc, 2 dc into foll dc*, rep once from *to* = 16 dc **Round 6** *1 dc into each of next 7 dc, 2 dc into foll dc*, rep once from *to* = 18 dc **Round 7** *1 dc into each of next 8 dc, 2 dc into foll dc*, rep once from *to* = 20 dc **Round 8** *1 dc into each of next 9 dc, 2 dc into foll dc*, rep once from *to* = 22 dc **Round 9** *1 dc into each of next 10 dc, 2 dc into foll dc*, rep once from *to* = 24 dc **Round 10** *1 dc into each of next 11 dc, 2 dc into foll dc*, rep once from *to* = 26 dc **Round 11** *1 dc into each of next 12 dc, 2 dc into foll dc*, rep once from *to* = 28 dc **Round 12** *1 dc into each of next 13 dc, 2 dc into foll dc*, rep once from *to* = 30 dc **Round 13** *1 dc into each of next 14 dc, 2 dc into foll dc*, rep once from *to* = 32 dc **Round 14** *1 dc into each of next 15 dc, 2 dc into foll dc*, rep once from *to* = 34 dc **Round 15** *1 dc into each of next 16 dc, 2 dc into foll dc*, rep once from *to* = 36 dc **Round 16** *1 dc into each of next 17 dc, 2 dc into foll dc*, rep once from *to* = 38 dc **Round 17** *1 dc into each of next 18 dc, 2 dc into foll dc*, rep once from *to* = 40 dc **Round 18** *1 dc into each of next 19 dc, 2 dc into foll dc*, rep once from *to* = 42 dc **Round 19** *1 dc into each of next 20 dc, 2 dc into foll dc*, rep once from *to* = 44 dc **Round 20** *1 dc into each of next 21 dc, 2 dc into foll dc*, rep once from *to* = 46 dc **Round 21** *1 dc into each of next 22 dc, 2 dc into foll dc*, rep once from *to* = 48 dc **Round 22–24** 1 dc into each dc to end Fix the eyes on round 19, spacing them out by 3 dc.

Fill with toy filling and continue to do so while working the next rounds.

**Round 25** *1 dc into each of next 4 dc, dc2tog, rep 7 times from to* = 40 dc **Round 26** *1 dc into each of next 3 dc, dc2tog, rep 7 times from to* = 32 dc **Round 27** *1 dc into each of next 2 dc, dc2tog, rep 7 times from to* = 24 dc **Round 28** *1 dc into next dc, dc2tog, rep 7 times from to* = 16 dc **Round 29** *dc2tog, rep 7 times from to* = 8 dc **Round 30** *dc2tog, rep 3 times from to* = 4 dc Fasten off. Weave the thread through all dc of last round, pull on yarn to close head, then fasten off.

## Body

With yarn A, make 48 ch. Work in rows.
**Row 1** 1 dc into 2nd ch from hook, 1 dc into each foll ch to end = 47 dc
**Rows 2–4** 1 ch, 1 dc into each dc to end **Row 5** dc2tog, 1 dc into each foll dc = 46 dc **Row 6** As row 5 = 45 dc
**Rows 7–8** 1 ch, 1 dc into each dc to end **Rows 9–16** Rep twice rows 5–8 = 41 dc **Rows 17–30** As row 5 = 27 dc
Fasten off.

## Bottom

With yarn A, make a magic ring.
Work in a spiral.
**Round 1** 8 dc into magic ring. Pull yarn to close ring.
**Round 2** 2 dc into each foll dc = 16 dc **Round 3** *1 dc into next dc, 2 dc into foll dc, rep 7 times from to* = 24 dc **Round 4** *1 dc into next 2 dc, 2 dc into foll dc, rep 7 times from to* = 32 dc **Round 5** *1 dc into next 3 dc, 2 dc into foll dc, rep 7 times from to* = 40 dc **Round 6** *1 dc into next 4 dc, 2 dc into foll dc, rep 7 times from to* = 48 dc **Rounds 7–9** 1 dc into each dc to end Work 1 ss into next dc to finish.
Fasten off.

## Arms (x 2)

With yarn B, make a magic ring.

Work in a spiral.

**Round 1** 6 dc into magic ring. Pull yarn to close ring.

**Round 2** 2 dc into each foll dc = 12 dc **Rounds 3–10** 1 dc into each dc to end Continue with yarn A.

**Rounds 11–38** 1 dc into each dc to end Work 1 ss into next dc to finish. Fasten off.

# Legs (x 2)

With yarn B, make a magic ring.

Work in a spiral.

**Round 1** 16 dc into magic ring. Pull yarn to close ring.

**Rounds 2–14** 1 dc into each dc to end Continue with yarn A.

**Rounds 15–32** 1 dc into each dc to end Work 1 ss into next dc to finish. Fasten off.

# Tail

Work as indicated for raccoon's tail, page. Make a magic ring and work first 16 rounds with yarn B, then continue with yarn A.

# Ears (x 2)

With yarn A, make 12 ch. Work in rows.

**Row 1** 1 dc into 2nd ch from hook, 1 dc into each foll ch = 11 dc **Row 2** dc2tog, 1 dc into each foll dc = 10 dc **Rows 3–8** As row 2 = 4 dc

**Row 9** dc2tog, rep once = 2 dc

**Row 10** dc2tog = 1 dc

Fasten off.

Make a similar piece with yarn B.

# Making up

Sew in the threads on the WS.

Sew the zip between the edges of the body. Sew row 1 of the body around the bottom. Sew the last round of the body to the head making sure the zip is centred at the front.

Fill the arms and legs with toy filling. Sew the arms to the body, just below the head. Sew the legs on the front part of the bottom, and the tail on the back part.

To make the ears, sew one piece made with yarn A onto a piece made with yarn B, sew to the head. Repeat with the other ear, spacing them out by 7 dc.

With the felting needle, apply the carded wool on rows 1–4 of the head to make the nose (see instructions page).

Photos on pages 31, 32 to 34 and 37

# *The koala*

## Materials for the koala
- Yarn 40% combed wool, 40% acrylic and 20% mohair for crochet hook 4mm: 2 skeins grey (yarn A)
- Yarn 100% acrylic for crochet hook 3.5mm: 1 skein black (yarn B)
- 2 solid eyes with shank backs, black, size 10mm (⅜in)
- Toy filling
- Crochet hook 4mm
- Scissors
- Wool needle

## Head, legs, torso and arms
With yarn A, work as indicated on page.

## Nose

## Nose

With yarn B, make 3 ch.

Work in a spiral.

**Round 1** 1 dc into 2nd ch from hook, 2 dc into last ch; on other side of foundation chain, 2 dc into next ch, 2 dc into first ch = 6 dc **Round 2** *1 dc into next dc, 2 dc into each of foll 2 dc*, rep once from *to* = 10 dc **Round 3** 1 dc into each of next 2 dc, 2 dc into each of foll 2 dc, 1 dc into each of next 3 dc, 2 dc into each of foll 2 dc, 1 dc into last dc = 14 dc **Round 4** 1 dc into each of next 3 dc, 2 dc into each of foll 2 dc, 1 dc into each of next 5 dc, 2 dc into each of foll 2 dc, 1 dc into each of last 2 dc = 18 dc **Round 5** 1 dc into each of next 4 dc, 2 dc into each of foll 2 dc, 1 dc into each of next 7 dc, 2 dc into each of foll 2 dc, 1 dc into each of last 3 dc = 22 dc **Round 6** 1 dc into each dc to end

Work 1 ss into next dc to finish.

Fasten off.

## Ears (x 2)

With yarn A, work as for head, to end of round 4 = 32 dc **Rounds 5–10** 1 dc into each dc to end Work 1 ss into next dc to finish.

Fasten off.

## Making up

Work as indicated on page.

Fix the eyes on row 11 of the head, spacing them out by 10 dc. Fill the nose with toy filling, then sew it under the eyes. Sew the ears on the head, rounding them at the base.

## Materials for sailor clothing

- Yarn 100% acrylic for crochet hook 3.5mm: 1 skein turquoise (yarn A), 1 skein off white (yarn B), 1 skein navy blue (yarn C), 1 skein red

(yarn D), 1 skein yellow (yarn E)
- 3 snap fasteners 10mm (⅜in)
- 1 button 10mm (⅜in)
- Sewing thread
- Crochet hook 4mm
- Wool needle
- Sewing kit

# Blouse

### Body
With yarn A, make 43 ch. Work in rows.
**Row 1** (RS) 1 dc into 2nd ch from hook, 1 dc into each foll ch to end = 42 dc **Row 2** 1 ch, 1 dc into each dc
**Rows 3–4** With yarn B, as row 2
**Rows 5–6** With yarn A, as row 2
**Rows 7–14** Rep rows 3–6 twice more

### Left back
**Row 15** With yarn B, 1 ch, 1 dc into each of next 10 dc, turn **Row 16** With yarn B, as row 2, working only on 10 dc **Rows 17–18** With yarn A, as row 16
**Rows 19–20** With yarn B, as row 16
**Rows 21–22** With yarn A, as row 16
Fasten off.

### Front
On RS, re-join yarn B in 12th dc of row 14.
**Row 15** 1 ch, 1 dc into dc where yarn was re-joined, 1 dc into each of next 19 dc, turn **Row 16** As row 2, working only on 20 dc **Rows 17–18** With yarn A, as row 16

**Rows 19–20** With yarn B, as row 16
**Row 21** With yarn A, dc2tog to end = 10 dc **Row 22** With yarn A, as row 2
Fasten off.

## Right back
On RS, re-join yarn B in 33rd dc of row 14.
**Row 15** 1 ch, 1 dc into dc where yarn was re-joined, 1 dc into each rem 9 dc **Row 16** As row 2, working only on 10 dc **Rows 17–18** With yarn A, as row 16
**Rows 19–20** With yarn B, as row 16
**Rows 21–22** With yarn A, as row 16
Fasten off.

## Sleeves
Sew the fronts and back together along 3 dc (armhole-side) to form the shoulders.

### Right sleeve
On RS, re-join yarn B in free dc at base of right armhole. Work in a spiral.
**Round 1** 1 ch, 1 dc into dc where yarn is re-joined, 1 dc into rows 15–22 from right back, 1 dc into rows 22–15 from front = 17 dc **Round 2** 1 dc into each dc to end
**Rounds 3–4** With yarn A, as round 2
**Rounds 5–6** With yarn B, as round 2
**Rounds 7–16** Rep rounds 3–6 twice, then work rounds 3–4
Work 1 ss into next dc to finish.
Fasten off.

### Left sleeve
As for right sleeve (on round 1, work on rows 15–22 from front then rows 22–15 from left back).

22–15 from left back.

## Finishing

Sew in the threads on the WS. Sew the snap fasteners on the back sides on rows 3, 11 and 19.

## Trousers

With yarn C, work as indicated for fox's trousers on page.
Fold 4 rounds upwards at the legs' hem.

## Scarf

With yarn D, make 71 ch.
1 dc into 2nd ch from hook, 1 dc into each next dc to end = 70 dc Fasten off.
Sew in the threads on the WS.

## Boots

With yarn E, work as indicated on page.
With yarn B, work 1 round of ss around the sole by inserting the hook into the free loop of dc from round 2.

### Variation

The koala's trousers have a slit in the back. If you prefer for them to be closed, follow the instructions for the butcher's trousers on page, by crocheting a total of 19 rounds for each leg.

Photos on pages 31 and 34 to 36

# *The panda*

## Materials for the panda

- Yarn 40% combed wool, 40% acrylic and 20% mohair for crochet hook 4mm: 2 skeins cream (yarn A)
- Yarn 100% acrylic for crochet hook 3.5mm: 1 skein black (yarn B)
- Black carded wool
- 2 solid eyes with shank backs, brown, size 10mm (⅜in)
- Toy filling
- Crochet hook 4mm
- Scissors
- Wool needle
- Felting needle

## Head, legs, torso and arms

Work as indicated on page. Work the head with yarn A and the legs with yarn B. Use yarn A for the first 18 rounds of torso, then yarn B for the rem 4 rounds. Use yarn B for the arms.

## Ears (x 2)

With yarn B, work as head to end of round 2 = 16 dc **Rounds 3–18** 1 dc into each dc to end Work 1 ss into next dc to finish.
Fasten off.

## Making up

Work as indicated on page

Before fixing the eyes, make two oval shapes with the carded wool and the felting needle: place them between rounds 12 and 17, across 4 dc at the widest part of the shape, spacing them out by 9 dc. Fix the eyes in the middle of the shapes. Sew the ears on the head.

For the nose, make a ball in carded wool and fix it under the eyes, then add below a vertical line to the base of the head (see instructions page

## Materials for clothing

- Yarn 100% acrylic for crochet hook 3.5mm: 1 skein off white (yarn A), 1 skein pink (yarn B)
- 4 snap fasteners 10mm (0.4in)
- Sewing thread
- Crochet hook 4mm
- Wool needle
- Sewing kit

## Dress

## Body

### Yoke and right sleeve

With yarn A, make 37 ch. Work in rows.

**Row 1** (RS) 1 dc into 2nd ch from hook, 1 dc into each foll ch to end = 36 dc **Row 2** With yarn B, 1 ch, 1 dc into each dc to end **Row 3** As row 2
**Rows 4–5** With yarn A, as row 2
**Row 6** With yarn B, as row 2

### Yoke and back of left sleeve

**Row 7** With yarn B, 1 ch, 1 dc into each of first 12 dc, 7 ch = 20 st **Row 8** With yarn A, 1 dc into 2nd ch from hook, 1 dc into each of next 6 ch, 1 dc into each of foll 12 dc = 18 dc **Row 9** With yarn A, 1 ch, 1 dc into each dc to end **Rows 10–11** With yarn B, as row 9
**Rows 12–13** As row 9
Fasten off.

### Yoke and left sleeve

With yarn B, make 7 ch. Work in rows.

**Row 7** 1 dc into 2nd ch from hook, 1 dc into each of the next 6 ch, 1 dc into 25th dc of row 6 (on RS), 1 dc into each of foll 11 dc = 18 dc **Rows 8–9** With yarn A, 1 ch, 1 dc into next dc to end **Rows 10–11** With yarn B, as rows 8–9
**Rows 12–13** As rows 8–9

### Arm closures

Fold the work in half, row 1 to row 13, WS to WS. With the back opening facing you, insert the hook through both layers with yarn A in 1st dc of left sleeve, work 1 ss in each of the first 12 dc.
Fasten off.

Turn the work so that the right sleeve is on your right. With the back opening still facing you, insert the hook through both layers with yarn A in

1st dc of right sleeve, work 1 ss in each of the first 12 dc.
Fasten off.

## Lower part

Turn the work so that the front of the dress is facing you and the left sleeve is on the right. On RS, re-join yarn B in 1st dc of row 13 of the yoke of the right back.

**Row 1** (RS) 1 ch, 1 dc into each of 6 dc of right yoke, 1 dc into closure of right sleeve, 1 dc into each of 12 dc of front yoke, 1 dc into closure of left sleeve, 1 dc into each of 6 dc or left yoke = 26 dc **Row 2** With yarn B, 1 ch, 1 dc into each dc to end **Row 3** With yarn A, 1 ch, 1 dc into each of first 7 dc, 3 dc into next dc, 1 dc into each of foll 10 dc, 3 dc into next dc, 1 dc into each of last 7 dc = 30 dc **Row 4** With yarn A, as row 2

**Row 5** With yarn B, 1 ch, 1 dc into each of first 8 dc, 3 dc into next dc, 1 dc into each of foll 12 dc, 3 dc into next dc, 1 dc into each of last 8 dc = 34 dc **Row 6** As row 2

**Row 7** With yarn A, 1 ch, 1 dc into each of first 9 dc, 3 dc into next dc, 1 dc into each of foll 14 dc, 3 dc into next dc, 1 dc into each of last 9 dc = 38 dc **Row 8** With yarn A, as row 2

**Row 9** With yarn B, as row 2

**Row 10** With yarn B, 1 ch, 1 dc into each of first 10 dc, 3 dc into next dc, 1 dc into each of foll 16 dc, 3 dc into next dc, 1 dc into each of last 10 dc = 42 dc **Rows 11–12** With yarn A, as row 2

**Row 13** With yarn B, 1 ch, 1 dc into each of first 11 dc, 3 dc into next dc, 1 dc into each of foll 18 dc, 3 dc into next dc, 1 dc into each of last 11 dc = 46 dc **Row 14** With yarn B, as row 2

**Row 15** With yarn A, as row 2

**Row 16** With yarn A, 1 ch, 1 dc into each of first 12 dc, 3 dc into next dc, 1 dc into each of foll 20 dc, 3 dc into next dc, 1 dc into each of last 12 dc = 50 dc **Rows 17–18** With yarn B, as row 2

**Row 19** With yarn A, 1 ch, 1 dc into each of first 13 dc, 3 dc into next dc, 1 dc into each of foll 22 dc, 3 dc into next dc, 1 dc into each of last 13 dc = 54 dc

## Edging

On the side of the work, 1 dc into each of rows 19–1 of lower part, 1 dc into each of 7 rows of yoke at left back, 1 dc into each of 6 dc of left back neckline, 1 dc into each of 12 dc of front neckline, 1 dc into each of 6 dc of right back neckline, 1 dc into each of 7 rows of yoke at right back, 1 dc into each of rows 1–18 of lower piece, 2 dc into row 19, 1 ss into 1st dc of row 19 = 77 dc.
Fasten off.

## Collar

### Left part
On RS, re-join yarn A in 1st dc of edge of neckline of left back.
**Row 1** 1 ch, 1 dc into each of first 12 dc, turn **Rows 2–7** 1 ch, 1 dc into each of 12 dc Fasten off.

### Right part
On RS, re-join yarn A in dc immediately after left part. Work as left part, work 7 rows of dc. Fasten off.

## Cuffs

On RS, re-join yarn A in 1st ss of sleeve closure (any side). Work in a spiral.
**Round 1** 1 ch, 2 dc into ss, 1 dc into each of the 13 rows of the sleeve = 15 dc **Rounds 2–15** 1 dc into each dc to end Work 1 ss into next dc to finish.
Fasten off.
Make second cuff the same way.

## Finishing

Sew in the threads on the WS. On each collar part, fold the vertical edge at the back in two outwards, fold back the collar at the front onto the front of the dress and maintain these folds with a few stitches. Fold the cuffs in two. Sew the snap fasteners on the back of the dress: on round 16 of lower part, on the collar and two others in between the first two, at regular intervals.

## Hat

With yarn B, work as for panda's head, to end of round 6 = 48 dc. **Round 7** *1 dc into each of next 23 dc, 2 dc into foll dc*, rep once from *to* = 50 dc
**Rounds 8–20** 1 dc into each dc to end Work 1 ss into next dc to finish.

## Visor

Turn. Continue in rows.
**Row 1** (RS 1 ch, 1 dc into each of first 25 dc, turn = 25 dc **Row 2** dc2tog, 1 dc into each foll dc = 24 dc **Rows 3–6** As row 2 = 20 dc

## Edge

Turn on the side, 1 dc into each of rows 6–1 of the visor, 1 dc into each free dc of round 20, 1 dc into each of rows 1–6 of visor, 1 dc into each 20 dc of row 6, 1 ss into 1st dc of edge = 57 dc.
Fasten off.
Sew in the threads on the WS.

## Boots

With yarn A, work as indicated on page by crocheting a total of 15 rounds.
Fold 3 rounds outwards.

Photos on pages 38 to 39

# *The pigs*

## Materials for the pigs

- Yarn 100% acrylic for crochet hook 3.5mm: 2 skein pink (for the chef, yarn A), light pink (for the butcher, yarn B), or dark pink (for the junior chef, yarn C)
- Carded wool, maroon
- 2 solid eyes with shank backs, maroon, size 10mm (⅜in) x 3 pigs
- Toy filling
- Crochet hook 4mm
- Scissors
- Wool needle
- Felting needle

## Head, legs, torso and arms

Work as indicated on page

## Snout

Work as for head, to end of round 4 = 32 dc.
**Rounds 5–9** 1 dc into each dc
Work 1 ss into next dc to finish.
Fasten off.

## Ears (x 2)

Make a magic ring. Work in a spiral.
**Round 1** 6 dc into magic ring. Pull yarn to close ring.
**Round 2** *1 dc into each of next 2 dc, 2 dc into foll dc*, rep once from *to* = 8 dc **Round 3** *1 dc into each of next 3 dc, 2 dc into foll dc*, rep once from *to* = 10 dc **Round 4** *1 dc into each of next 4 dc, 2 dc into foll dc*, rep once from *to* = 12 dc **Round 5** *1 dc into each of next 5 dc, 2 dc into foll dc*, rep once from *to* = 14 dc **Round 6** *1 dc into each of next 6 dc, 2 dc into foll dc*, rep once from *to* = 16 dc **Round 7** *1 dc into each of next 7 dc, 2 dc into foll dc*, rep once from *to* = 18 dc **Rounds 8–9** 1 dc into each dc to end Work 1 ss into next dc to finish.
Fasten off.

## Making up

Work as indicated on page.

Fix the eyes on round 12 of the head spacing them out by 10 dc.

Fill the snout with toy filling then sew it at the base of the eyes, aligning with the penultimate round of head. Using the felting needle make two nostrils with the carded wool, placing them between rounds 4 and 6 (see instructions page. Sew the ears on the head, rounding them slightly.

### Note

The clothing for the three pigs are explained on pages 81 to 84. Don't hesitate to interchange them as you wish: an apron and a chef's hat or heeled shoes, an undershirt and a cap…

Photos on pages 39, 40 to 41 and 46

# The chef

## Materials for chef's clothing

- Yarn 100% acrylic for crochet hook 3.5mm: 1 skein white (yarn A), 1 skein black (yarn B)
- 3 snap fasteners 10mm (⅜in)
- 1 button 10mm (⅜in)
- Sewing thread
- Crochet hook 4mm
- Wool needle
- Sewing kit

## Vest

### Body
With yarn A, make 41 ch. Work in rows.

**Row 1** (RS) 1 dc into 2nd ch from hook, 1 dc into each foll ch = 40 dc
**Row 2** 1 ch, 1 dc into each dc to end
**Rows 3–16** As row 2

## Right front
**Row 17** 1 ch, 1 dc into each of first 11 dc, turn **Rows 18–24** As row 2, working only on 11 dc Fasten off.

## Back
On RS, re-join yarn A in 13th dc of row 16.
**Row 17** 1 ch, 1 dc in dc where yarn was re-joined, 1 dc into each of foll 15 dc, turn **Rows 18–24** As row 2, working only on central 16 dc Fasten off.

## Right front
On RS, re-join yarn A in 20th dc of row 16.
**Row 17** 1 ch, 1 dc in dc where yarn was re-joined, 1 dc into each of rem 10 dc, turn **Rows 18–24** As row 2, working only on 11 dc Fasten off.

## Collar
On RS, re-join yarn A in 4th dc of row 24.
**Row 1** (RS) 1 ch, 1 dc into dc where yarn was re-joined, 1 dc into each of next 7 dc, 1 ch, 1 dc into each foll 16 dc from back, 1 ch, 1 dc into each of foll 8 dc from left front, turn = 34 st **Row 2** 1 ch, 1 dc into each st = 34 dc
**Rows 3–5** 1 ch, 1 dc into each dc to end
Fasten off.

## Sleeves

## Right sleeve
On RS, re-join yarn A in free dc at the base of the right armhole. Work in

a spiral.

**Round 1** 1 ch, 1 dc into dc where yarn was re-joined, 1 dc into row 1–8 of back, 1 dc into ch from collar, 1 dc into rows 8–1 from right front = 18 dc **Rounds 2–22** 1 dc into each dc to end

Work 1 ss into next dc to finish.

Fasten off.

### Left sleeve

Work as for right sleeve (on round 1, work on rows 1–8 of left front first, then on rows 8–1 of back).

### Finishing

Sew in the threads on the WS. Fold the collar on itself (RS to RS) and fix it with a few stitches. Sew the snap fasteners on the fronts on rows 5, 14 and 23. Fold up the sleeves by 4 rounds.

## Trousers

Work with yarn A.

### Left leg

Make 18 ch, join with a ss to form ring.

Work in a spiral.

**Round 1** 1 ch, 1 dc into same ch, 1 dc into each foll ch to end = 18 dc
**Rounds 2–22** 1 dc into each dc to end

Fasten off.

### Right leg

As for left leg, without cutting the yarn at the end.

### Top part

Work in a spiral.

**Round 1** 3 ch at the end of right leg, 1 dc into each dc of left leg, 3 ch, 1 dc into each dc of right leg = 42 st **Round 2** *1 dc into each 3 ch, 1 dc into each foll 18 dc*, rep once from *to* = 42 dc **Rounds 3–4** 1 dc into each dc to end

Work 1 ss into next dc (to arrive 1 dc before the middle of the back). Turn. Continue in rows.

**Row 1** (WS) 1 ch, 1 dc into each of next 41 dc, turn = 41 dc **Row 2** 1 ch, 1 dc into each of first 9 dc, dc2tog, 1 dc into each foll 19 dc, dc2tog, 1 dc into last 9 dc = 39 dc **Rows 3–6** 1 ch, 1 dc into each dc to end

At end of row 6, make 20 ch.

Fasten off.

Re-join yarn A in 1st dc of row 6, make 20 ch, then cut the yarn and fasten off.

## Finishing

Sew in the threads on the WS. Close the crotch with 3 small whip stitches. Fold 4 rounds of the legs' hem outwards. Tie the two chains together in a bow at the waist (at the back).

## Chef's hat

With yarn A, make 20 ch, join with a ss to form a ring.

Work in a spiral.

**Round 1** 1 ch, 1 dc into same ch, 1 dc into each foll ch to end = 20 dc
**Rounds 2–12** 1 dc into each dc to end
**Round 13** 2 dc into each dc to end = 40 dc **Rounds 14–22** 1 dc into each dc to end

Fasten off.

Weave the thread through all dc of last round, pull on yarn to close hat, then fasten off.

## Finishing
Sew in the threads on the WS. Fold the last 4 rounds of the hat outwards.

## Bow tie
With yarn B, make 11 ch. Work in rows.
**Row 1** 1 dc into 2nd ch from hook, 1 dc into each foll ch = 10 dc **Rows 2–5** 1 ch, 1 dc into each dc to end
Fasten off.

## Finishing
Sew in the threads on the WS.

Wrap yarn B several times around the crocheted rectangle to tighten the middle.

Sew the bow tie on one of the vest's fronts.

Photos on pages 38, 42 to 43 and 46

# *The butcher*

## Materials for butcher's clothing
- Yarn 100% acrylic for crochet hook 3.5mm: 1 skein off white
- Crochet hook 4mm
- Scissors
- Wool needle

## Undershirt
Make 40 ch, join with a ss to form a ring.

Work in a spiral.

**Round 1** 1 ch, 1 dc into same ch, 1 dc into each foll ch = 40 dc **Rounds 2–11** 1 dc into each dc to end **Round 12** 1 dc into each of next 9 dc, dc2tog, 1 dc into each foll 18 dc, dc2tog, 1 dc into each rem 9 dc = 38 dc

**Round 13** 1 dc into each of next 9 dc, dc2tog, 1 dc into each foll 16 dc, dc2tog, 1 dc into each rem 9 dc = 36 dc **Round 14** 1 dc into each of next 8 dc, dc2tog, 1 dc into each foll 16 dc, dc2tog, 1 dc into each rem 8 dc = 34 dc **Round 15** 1 dc into each of next 8 dc, dc2tog, 1 dc into each foll 14 dc, dc2tog, 1 dc into each rem 8 dc = 32 dc **Round 16** 1 dc into each of next 7 dc, dc2tog, 1 dc into each foll 14 dc, dc2tog, 1 dc into each rem 7 dc = 30 dc **Round 17** 1 dc into each of next 7 dc, dc2tog, 1 dc into each foll 12 dc, dc2tog, 1 dc into each rem 7 dc = 28 dc **Round 18** 1 dc into each of next 4 dc, *7 ch, skip 6 dc*, 1 dc into each foll 8 dc, rep once from *to* , 1 dc into each of rem 4 dc = 16 dc and 2 loops of 7 ch each for the shoulder straps.
**Round 19** 1 dc into each st
Fasten off.
Sew in the threads on the WS.

# Trousers

### Leg 1
Work 18 ch, join with a ss to form a ring.
Work in a spiral.
**Round 1** 1 ch, 1 dc into same ch, 1 dc into each foll ch = 18 dc **Rounds 2–10** 1 dc into each dc to end Fasten off.

### Leg 2
As for Leg 1, without cutting the yarn at the end.

### Top part
Work in a spiral.
**Round 1** 4 ch at the end of leg 2, 1 dc into each dc of leg 1, 4 ch, 1 dc into each dc of leg 2 = 44 st **Round 2** *1 dc into each 4 ch, 1 dc into each*

*foll 18 dc*, rep once from *to* = 44 dc **Rounds 3–11** 1 dc into each dc to end Work 1 ss into next dc to finish.
Fasten off.

**Finishing**

Sew in the threads on the WS.
Close the crotch with 4 small whip stitches.
On the last round, in the middle of the front, fix two long threads of yarn and knot them with a bow.

## Heeled shoes
Work as indicated on page.

Photos on pages 39, 44 to 45 and 47

# The junior chef

## Materials for clothing
- Yarn 100% acrylic for crochet hook 3.5mm: 1 skein blue
- 1 small safety pin
- Crochet hook 4mm
- Scissors
- Wool needle

## Apron

**Body**
Make 35 ch. Work in rows.
**Row 1** (RS) 1 dc into 2nd ch from hook, 1 dc into each foll ch = 34 dc
**Rows 2–14** 1 ch, 1 dc into each dc to end **Rows 15** dc2tog, 1 dc into

each foll dc until 2 dc from end of row, dc2tog = 32 dc **Rows 16–26** As row 15 = 10dc
**Rows 27–33** 1 ch, 1 dc into each dc to end

## Edging

Turn on side of work, 1 dc into each of rows 33–15 (armhole), 2 dc into row 14, 1 dc into each of rows 13–1, 2 dc into 1st dc of row 1, 1 dc into each of foll 32 dc, 2 dc into last dc, 1 dc into each of rows 1–13, 2 dc into row 14, 1 dc into each of rows 15–33 (armhole), 22 ch = 104 dc and 22 ch.
Fasten off.
Re-join the yarn in other side of edging and make 22 ch. Fasten off.

## Pocket

Make 10 ch. Work in rows.
**Row 1** (RS) 1 dc into 2nd ch from hook, 1 dc into each foll ch = 9 dc
**Rows 2–5** 1 ch, 1 dc into each dc to end **Row 6** dc2tog, 1 dc into each foll dc = 8 dc **Rows 7–9** As row 6 = 5 dc
Fasten off.

## Edging

On RS, re-join the yarn in last dc of row 1. 1 ch, 1 dc into rows 1–9, 1 dc into each 5 dc of row 9, 1 dc into rows 9–1, 1 ss into ch = 24 st Fasten off.

## Finishing

Sew in the threads on the WS.
Sew the pocket on the front of the body, in the middle, aligned with row 9. Tie the two chains of the apron together with a bow. Close the back of the apron with the safety pin.

## Cap

Work as for head of pig (see page), to end round 3 = 24 dc.
**Round 4** 1 dc into back loop of each dc **Rounds 5–9** 1 dc into each dc to end Work 1 ss into next dc to finish.

## Visor

Turn. Continue in rows.
**Round 1** (WS 1 ch, 1 dc into each of next 10 dc, turn = 10 dc **Round 2** dc2tog, 1 dc into each foll 8 dc = 9 dc **Row 3** dc2tog, 1 dc into each foll 7 dc = 8 dc **Row 4** dc2tog, 1 dc into each of foll 4 dc, dc2tog = 6 dc Fasten off.

Sew in the threads on the WS.

## Flat shoes

Work as indicated on page.

Photos on pages 38 to 39, 42, 44 and 47

# The meat

## Materials for leg of lamb
- Yarn 40% combed wool, 40% acrylic and 20% mohair for crochet hook 4mm: 1 skein cream (yarn A), 1 skein beige (yarn B), 1 skein dark red (yarn C)
- 1 small safety pin
- Toy filling
- Crochet hook 4mm
- Scissors
- Wool needle

## Main part
With yarn A, make a magic ring.
Work in a spiral.
**Round 1** 10 dc into magic ring. Pull yarn to close ring.

**Rounds 2–4** 1 dc into each dc to end **Round 5** *1 dc into each of next 3 dc, dc2tog, rep once from to* = 8 dc **Round 6** *1 dc into each of next 2 dc, dc2tog, rep once from to* = 6 dc **Rounds 7–9** 1 dc into each dc to end
Continue with yarn B
**Round 10** *1 dc into next dc, 2 dc into next dc, rep twice from to* = 9 dc
**Round 11** *1 dc into each of next 2 dc, 2 dc into next dc, rep twice from to* = 12 dc **Round 12** *1 dc into each of next 3 dc, 2 dc into next dc, rep twice from to* = 15 dc **Round 13** *1 dc into each of next 4 dc, 2 dc into next dc, rep twice from to* = 18 dc **Round 14** *1 dc into each of next 5 dc, 2 dc into next dc, rep twice from to* = 21 dc **Round 15** *1 dc into each of next 6 dc, 2 dc into next dc, rep twice from to* = 24 dc **Round 16** *1 dc into each of next 7 dc, 2 dc into next dc, rep twice from to* = 27 dc **Round 17** *1 dc into each of next 8 dc, 2 dc into next dc, rep twice from to* = 30 dc **Rounds 18–24** 1 dc into each dc to end Cut the yarn and fasten off

### Sliced end

With yarn A, make a magic ring.
Work in a spiral.
**Round 1** 8 dc into magic ring. Pull yarn to close ring.
Continue with yarn B.
**Round 2** *2 dc into each dc* = 16 dc **Round 3** *1 dc into next dc, 2 dc into each foll dc, rep 7 times from to* = 24 dc **Round 4** *1 dc into each of next 3 dc, 2 dc into each foll dc, rep 5 times from to* = 30 dc **Round 5** 1 dc into each dc to end Work 1ss into next dc to finish.
Fasten off.

### Finishing

Sew in the threads on the WS. Fill with toy filling then sew the last round around the sliced part.

## Materials for the sausages

- Yarn 100% acrylic for crochet hook 3.5mm: 1 skein dark pink
- Toy filling
- Crochet hook 4mm
- Scissors
- Wool needle

## Sausage

Make a magic ring.

Work in a spiral.

**Round 1** 3 dc into magic ring. Pull yarn to close ring.

**Rounds 2–14** 1 dc into each dc Work 1 ss into next dc to finish.

Fill with toy filling.

Fasten off.

Weave the yarn through all dc of last round, pull on yarn to close the sausage, fasten off.

## Finishing

Sew in the threads on the WS.

Make several sausages then sew them together.

## Materials for the roast

- Yarn 100% acrylic for crochet hook 3.5mm: 1 skein red (yarn A), 1 skein white (yarn B)
- Toy filling
- Crochet hook 4mm
- Scissors
- Wool needle

**Meat**

With yarn A, make a magic ring.

Work in a spiral.

**Round 1** 8 dc into magic ring. Pull yarn to close ring.

**Round 2** 2 dc into each dc = 16 dc **Round 3** *1 dc into each of next 3 dc, 2 dc into foll dc*, rep 3 times from *to* = 20 dc **Round 4** 1 dc into each dc to end **Round 5** 1 dc into back loop of each dc **Rounds 6–14** As round 4

**Round 15** As round 5

**Round 16** As round 4

Fill with toy filling.

**Round 17** *1 dc into each of next 3 dc, dc2tog*, rep 3 times from *to* = 16 dc **Round 18** dc2tog to end = 8 dc Work 1 ss into next dc to finish.

Fasten off.

Weave the yarn through all dc of last round, pull on yarn to close the roast, fasten off.

## Outer layer

With yarn B, make 37 ch. Work in rows.

**Row 1** 1 dc into 2nd ch from hook, 1 dc into each foll ch = 36 dc **Rows 2–5** 1 ch, 1 dc into each dc to end Fasten off.

## Finishing

Sew in the threads on the WS.

Close the bard in a loop by sewing the short edges together then place it around the meat.

Tie up the roast with yarn B.

Photos on pages 49 to 51 and 53

# *The bunny*

## Materials for the bunny
- Yarn 100% acrylic for crochet hook 3.5mm: 2 skeins off white
- Carded wool, pink
- 2 solid eyes with shank backs, matt black, size 10mm (⅜in)
- Toy filling
- Crochet hook 4mm
- Scissors
- Wool needle
- Felting needle

## Head
Work as indicated on page, to end of round 22 = 24 dc.

**Round 23** *1 dc into next dc, dc2tog*, rep 7 times from *to* = 16 dc Work 1 ss into next dc to finish.
Fasten off.

## Legs and torso

Work as indicated on page, to end of round 2 of torso = 32 dc. **Rounds 3–14** 1 dc into each dc to end
**Round 15** 1 dc into each of next 9 dc, dc2tog, 1 dc into each of foll 14 dc, dc2tog, 1 dc into each of last 5 dc = 30 dc **Round 16** 1 dc into each of next 9 dc, dc2tog, 1 dc into each of foll 12 dc, dc2tog, 1 dc into each of last 5 dc = 28 dc **Round 17** 1 dc into each of next 8 dc, dc2tog, 1 dc into each of foll 12 dc, dc2tog, 1 dc into each of last 4 dc = 26 dc **Round 18** 1 dc into each of next 8 dc, dc2tog, 1 dc into each of foll 10 dc, dc2tog, 1 dc into each of last 4 dc = 24 dc **Round 19** 1 dc into each of next 7 dc, dc2tog, 1 dc into each of foll 10 dc, dc2tog, 1 dc into each of last 3 dc = 22 dc **Round 20** 1 dc into each of next 7 dc, dc2tog, 1 dc into each of foll 8 dc, dc2tog, 1 dc into each of last 3 dc = 20 dc **Round 21** 1 dc into each of next 6 dc, dc2tog, 1 dc into each of foll 8 dc, dc2tog, 1 dc into each of last 2 dc = 18 dc **Round 22** 1 dc into each of next 6 dc, dc2tog, 1 dc into each of foll 6 dc, dc2tog, 1 dc into each of last 2 dc = 16 dc Work 1 ss into next dc to finish.
Fasten off.

## Ears (x2)

Make a magic ring.
Work in a spiral.
**Round 1** 6 dc into magic ring. Pull yarn to close ring.
**Round 2** *1 dc into each of next 2 dc, 2 dc into foll dc*, rep once from *to* = 8 dc **Round 3*** 1 dc into each of next 3 dc, 2 dc into foll dc*, rep once

from *to* = 10 dc **Round 4** *1 dc into each of next 4 dc, 2 dc into foll dc*, rep once from *to* = 12 dc **Round 5** *1 dc into each of next 5 dc, 2 dc into foll dc*, rep once from *to* = 14 dc **Round 6** *1 dc into each of next 6 dc, 2 dc into foll dc*, rep once from *to* = 16 dc **Rounds 7–20** 1 dc into each dc to end

Work 1 ss into next dc to finish.
Fasten off.

## Arms
Work as indicated on page.

## Making up
Work as indicated on page.

Fix the eyes on round 14 of the head, spacing them out by 10 dc.

With the felting needle, make a triangular nose with the carded wool, between rounds 16 and 18 (see instructions page.)

Sew the ears on the head, pinching them at the base.

## Materials for pink clothing
- Yarn 100% acrylic for crochet hook 3.5mm: 1 skein pink
- 40cm (15.75in) pink ribbon 40mm (1.5in) wide
- Crochet hook 4mm
- Wool needle

## Overall

### Leg 1
Make 16 ch and join wih a ss to make a ring.
Work in a spiral.

**Round 1** 1 ch, 1 dc into same ch, 1 dc into each foll ch = 16 dc **Rounds 2–8** 1 dc into each dc to end
Cut the yarn and fasten off

## Leg 2
As 1st leg, without cutting the yarn at the end

## Top part
Work in a spiral.
**Round 1** 4 ch at end of leg 2, 1 dc into each dc of leg 1, 4 ch, 1 dc into each dc of leg 2 = 40 dc **Round 2** *1 dc into each of 4 ch, 1 dc into each of foll 16 dc*, rep once from *to* = 40 dc **Rounds 3–8** 1 dc into each dc to end **Round 9** 1 dc into each of next 12 dc, dc2tog, 1 dc into each of foll 16 dc, dc2tog, 1 dc into each of last 8 dc = 38 dc **Round 10** 1 dc into each of next 11 dc, dc2tog, 1 dc into of foll 16 dc, dc2tog, 1 dc into each of last 7 dc = 36 dc **Round 11** 1 dc into each of next 11 dc, dc2tog, 1 dc into of foll 14 dc, dc2tog, 1 dc into each of last 7 dc = 34 dc **Round 12** 1 dc into each of next 10 dc, dc2tog, 1 dc into of foll 14 dc, dc2tog, 1 dc into each of last 6 dc = 32 dc **Round 13** 1 dc into each of next 10 dc, dc2tog, 1 dc into of foll 12 dc, dc2tog, 1 dc into each of last 6 dc = 30 dc **Round 14** 1 dc into each of next 9 dc, dc2tog, 1 dc into of foll 12 dc, dc2tog, 1 dc into each of last 5 dc = 28 dc **Round 15** 1 dc into each of next 9 dc, dc2tog, 1 dc into of foll 10 dc, dc2tog, 1 dc into each of last 5 dc = 26 dc **Round 16** 1 dc into each of next 7 dc, 11 ch, skip 6 dc, 1 dc into each of foll 4 dc, 11 ch, skip 6 dc, 1 dc into each of last 3 dc = 14 dc and 2 loops of 11 ch for shoulder straps **Round 17** 1 dc into each st
Fasten off.

## Finishing
Sew in the threads on the WS.

Close the crotch with 4 small whip stitches. Fold 2 rounds of the legs' hem outwards.

## Cardigan

### Right front
Make 19 ch. Work in rows.
**Row 1** (RS) 1 dc into 2nd ch from hook, 1 dc into each of next 7 ch, 1 tr into each of last 10 ch = 8 dc and 10 tr **Row 2** 3 ch (=1 tr), skip 1 tr at base of 3ch, 1 tr into each of next 9 tr, 1 dc into each dc to end **Row 3** 1 ch, 1 dc into each dc, 1 tr into each tr **Rows 4–6** Rep rows 2–3 once, then rep row 2

### Back
**Row 7** 1 ch, 1 dc into next dc, 7 ch, skip 7 dc, 1 tr into each tr **Row 8** 3 ch, skip 1tr at base of 3ch, 1 tr into each of foll 9 tr, 1 dc into each of 7 ch, 1 dc into last dc **Row 9** As row 3
**Row 10** As row 2
**Rows 11–20** Rep rows 9–10 5 times

### Left front
**Row 21** As row 7
**Row 22** As row 8
**Row 23** As row 3
**Row 24** As row 2
**Rows 25–27** Rep rows 23–24 once, rep row 23
Fasten off.

### Edging
Make 20 ch. On RS, 1 dc into each of 27 rows of neckline, 20 ch.
Fasten off.

## Finishing

Sew in the threads on the WS.

Make a knot with the 2 chains from neckline.

Tie a ribbon in a bow around the neck of the bunny.

## Slippers (x2)

Make 5 ch. Work in rows.

**Row 1** 1 dc into 2nd ch from hook, 1 dc into each foll ch = 4 dc **Rows 2–6** 1 ch, 1 dc into each dc

Continue in a spiral.

**Round 1** Turn on the side, 1 dc into rows 5–1, turn on the foundation chain, 1 dc into each 4 ch, turn on side, 1 dc into rows 1–5, turn on row 6, 1 dc into each of 4 dc = 18 dc **Round 2** 1 dc into back loop of each dc **Round 3** tr2tog, 1 dc into each of next 10 dc, (tr2tog) 3 times Fasten off. Sew in threads on WS.

## Materials for basket

- Yarn 100% acrylic for crochet hook 3.5mm: 1 skein pink

- 120x120mm (4.75x4.75in) pink vichy fabric
- Sewing thread
- Crochet hook 4mm
- Wool needle
- Sewing kit
- Iron

**Bottom**

Make a magic ring.

Work in rounds that are joined.

**Round 1** 4 ch (=1 tr + 1 ch), *3 tr into magic ring, 1 ch*, rep twice from *to* , 2 tr into magic ring, pull yarn to close ring, 1 ss into 3rd ch from beg

**Round 2** 4 ch (=1 tr + 1 ch), 3 tr into 1st 1 ch-sp, *1 ch, 3 tr, 1 ch, 3tr into foll 1 ch-sp*, rep twice from *to* , 1 ch, 2 tr into 1st 1 ch-sp, 1 ss into 3rd ch from beg **Round 3** 4 ch (=1 tr + 1 ch), 3 tr into 1st 1 ch-sp, °*1 ch, 3 tr into foll 1 ch-sp, 1 ch*°, *3 tr, 1 ch, 3tr into foll 1 ch-sp*, rep twice from *to* , rep once from ° to °, 2 tr into 1st 1 ch-sp, 1 ss into 3rd ch from beg **Round 4** 4 ch (=1 tr + 1 ch), 3 tr into 1st 1 ch-sp, °*1 ch, 3 tr into foll 1 ch-sp* °, *rep once from ° to* °, *1 ch, 3 tr, 1 ch, 3tr into foll 1 ch-sp*, rep twice from *to* , rep twice from ° to °, 1 ch, 2 tr into 1st 1 ch-sp, 1 ss into 3rd ch from beg **Round 5** 4 ch (=1 tr + 1 ch), 3 tr into 1st 1 ch-sp, °*1 ch, 3 tr into foll 1 ch-sp* °, *rep twice from ° to* °, *1 ch, 3 tr, 1 ch, 3tr into foll 1 ch-sp*, rep twice from *to* , rep 3 times from ° to °, 1 ch, 2 tr into 1st 1 ch-sp, 1 ss into 3rd ch

from beg

## Walls
**Round 6** 1 ch, 1 dc into each tr, 1 ss into 1st ch = 60 dc **Round 7** 1 ch, dc2tog to end, 1 ss into 1st ch = 30 dc **Round 8** 1 ch, dc2tog to end, 1 ss into 1st ch = 15 dc **Round 9** 1 ch, 1 dc into each foll ch to end

## Handles
**Round 10** 1 ch, 1 dc into 1st dc, 15 ch, skip 6 dc, 1 dc into each of next 9 dc, 15 ch, skip 6 dc, 1 dc into each of foll 8 dc, 1 ss into 1st ch **Round 11** 1 ch, 1 dc into each st, 1 ss into 1st ch Cut the yarn and fasten off.

## Finishing
Sew in the threads on the WS.
Fold 5mm (¼in) inwards at the edges of the vichy fabric and iron. Sew the fabric with slip stitches inside the basket.

> ### Note
> The bottom of the basket (the first 5 rounds) is worked exactly as a

simple granny square.

## Materials for ice cream cone

- Yarn 40% combed wool, 40% acrylic and 20% mohair for crochet hook 4mm: 1 skein beige (yarn A)
- Yarn 100% acrylic for crochet hook 3.5mm: 1 skein yellow (yarn B)
- 1 red bead 15mm (⅝in)
- Toy filling
- Sewing thread
- Crochet hook 4mm
- Wool needle
- Sewing kit

## Cone

With yarn A, make a magic ring.

Work in a spiral.

**Round 1** 6 dc into magic ring. Pull yarn to close ring.

**Round 2** *1 dc into each of next 2 dc, 2 dc into each foll dc, rep once from to = 8 dc* **Round 3** *1 dc into each of next 3 dc, 2 dc into each foll dc, rep once from to = 10 dc* **Round 4** *1 dc into each of next 4 dc, 2 dc into each foll dc, rep once from to = 12 dc* **Round 5** *1 dc into each of next 5 dc, 2 dc into each foll dc, rep once from to = 14 dc* **Round 6** *1 dc into each of next 6 dc, 2 dc into each foll dc, rep once from to = 16 dc* **Round 7** *1 dc into each of next 7 dc, 2 dc into each foll dc, rep once from to = 18 dc* **Round 8** *1 dc into each of next 8 dc, 2 dc into each foll dc, rep once from to = 20 dc* **Rounds 9-11** 1 dc into each dc to end

Work 1 ss in foll dc to finish.

Fasten off.

## Ice cream scoop

With yarn B, make a magic ring.

Work in a spiral.

**Round 1** 8 dc into magic ring. Pull yarn to close ring.

**Round 2** 2 dc into each dc = 16 dc

**Round 3** *1 dc into next dc, 2 dc into foll dc*, rep 7 times from *to* = 24 dc

**Rounds 4–9** 1 dc into each dc to end

**Round 10** 1 ss, 3 ch (=1 tr), 2 tr into next dc, °*skip 1 dc, 1 dc into next dc*°, skip 1 dc, 3 tr into next dc, rep 4 times from *to* , rep once from ° to °. Fasten off.

## Finishing

Sew in the threads on the WS.

Sew the bead on top of the scoop. Fill the cone and the scoop with toy filling. Insert cone into scoop, sew with small discreet stitches under the last round.

### *Variations*

Strawberry, vanilla, pistachio ice cream… it's up to you to choose the yarn colour that matches your favourite flavour. For those with a sweet tooth, you can even crochet the first two rounds of the cone in chocolate colour!

Photos on pages 50 to 53

# *The baby rabbit*

## Materials for the baby rabbit
- Yarn 100% acrylic for crochet hook 3.5mm: 1 skein off white (yarn A), 1 skein pink (yarn B)
- Carded wool, pink
- 2 solid eyes with shank backs, matt black, size 8mm ($5/16$in)
- Toy filling
- Crochet hook 4mm
- Pink felt-tip pen solvent-free
- Scissors
- Wool needle

## Head
With yarn A, make a magic ring.

Work in a spiral.

**Round 1** 8 dc into magic ring. Pull yarn to close ring.

**Round 2** 2 dc into each dc to end = 16 dc **Round 3** *1 dc into next dc, 2 dc into next dc*, rep 7 times from *to* = 24 dc **Round 4** *1 dc into each of next 2 dc, 2 dc into next dc*, rep 7 times from *to* = 32 dc **Rounds 5–14** 1 dc into each dc to end

**Round 15** *1 dc into each of next 2 dc, dc2tog*, rep 7 times from *to* = 24 dc **Round 16** *1 dc into next dc, dc2tog*, rep 7 times from *to* = 16 dc

**Round 17** dc2tog to end = 8 dc

Work 1 ss into the next dc to finish.

Fasten off.

## Legs and torso

Work with yarn B.

### Leg 1

Make a magic ring. Work in a spiral.

**Round 1** 8 dc into magic ring. Pull yarn to close ring.

**Rounds 2–18** 1 dc into each dc to end

Fasten off.

### Leg 2

As for Leg 1, without cutting the yarn at the end.

### Torso

Work in a spiral.

**Round 1** 2 ch at the end of leg 2, 1 dc into each dc of leg 1, 2 ch, 1 dc into each dc of leg 2 = 20 st Fill the legs with toy filling.

**Round 2** *1 dc into each of next 2 ch, 1 dc into each of foll dc*, rep once from *to* = 20 dc **Rounds 3–10** 1 dc into each dc to end

**Round 11** 1 dc into each of next 4 dc, (dc2tog) twice, 1 dc into each foll 6 dc, (dc2tog) twice, 1 dc into each of last 2 dc = 16 dc **Round 12** 1 dc into each of next 3 dc, (dc2tog) twice, 1 dc into each foll 4 dc, (dc2tog) twice, 1 dc into last dc = 12 dc **Round 13** 1 dc into each of next 2 dc, (dc2tog) twice, 1 dc into each foll 2 dc, (dc2tog) twice = 8 dc Work 1 ss into the next dc to finish.

Fasten off.

## Arms (x2

With yarn A, make a magic ring.

Work in a spiral.

**Round 1** 6 dc into magic ring. Pull yarn to close ring.

**Rounds 2–4** 1 dc into each dc to end

**Rounds 5–16** With yarn B, 1 dc into each dc to end Work 1 ss into the next dc to finish.

Fasten off.

## Ears (x2)

With yarn A, make a magic ring.

Work in a spiral.

**Round 1** 4 dc into magic ring. Pull yarn to close ring.

**Round 2** *1 dc into next dc, 2 dc into foll dc*, rep once from *to* = 6 dc **Round 3** *1 dc into each of next 2 dc, 2 dc into foll dc*, rep once from *to* = 8 dc

**Round 4** *1 dc into each of next 3 dc, 2 dc into foll dc*, rep once from *to* = 10 dc **Round 5** *1 dc into each of next 4 dc, 2 dc into foll dc*, rep once from *to* = 12 dc **Rounds 6–15** 1 dc into each dc to end

Work 1 ss into the next dc to close the ring.

Fasten off.

## Making up

Sew in the threads on the WS.

Close the crotch with 2 small whip stitches. Fill the torso with toy filling. Fix the eyes on round 11 of the head, spacing them out by 7 dc. Fill the head with toy filling then sew it to the torso, stich by stitch. Sew the arms to the torso, immediately under the head. Sew the ears to the head, pinching them at the base. Embroider a big cross stitch with yarn B to make the mouth. Apply some pink felt-tip pen to colour the cheeks.

## Materials for hat

- Yarn 100% acrylic for crochet hook 3.5mm: 1 skein pink
- Crochet hook 4mm
- Scissors
- Wool needle

Make a magic ring.
Work in a spiral.
**Round 1** 8 dc into magic ring. Pull yarn to close ring.
**Round 2** 2 dc into each dc = 16 dc
**Round 3** *1 dc into next dc, 2 dc into foll dc*, rep 7 times from *to* = 24 dc
**Round 4** *1 dc into each of next 2 dc, 2 dc into foll dc*, rep 7 times from *to* = 32 dc **Round 5** *1 dc into each of next 15 dc, 2 dc into foll dc*, rep once from *to* = 34 dc **Rounds 6–9** 1 dc into each dc to end

### Slits for the ears
**Round 10** 1 dc into each of next 14 dc, *5 ch, skip 5 dc, 1 dc into each of foll 5 dc*, rep once from *to* **Round 11** 1 dc into each st

### Ties
Turn. Continue in rows.

**Row 1** (RS) 1 ch, 1 dc into each of next 25 dc, turn **Row 2** 1 ch, 1 dc into each of next 25 dc, 29 ch, turn **Row 3** 1 dc into 2nd dc from hook, 1 dc into each of next 28 ch, 1 ss into next dc Fasten off.

On the RS, re-join the yarn in 1st dc of row 2. Make 29 ch, skip 1 ch, 1 dc into each of next 28 ch, 1 ss into foll dc.

Fasten off.

Sew in the threads on the WS.

## Materials for carrot crib

- Yarn 100% acrylic for crochet hook 3.5mm: 1 skein orange (yarn A), 1 skein green (yarn B)
- 1 orange zip 22cm (8½in) long
- Sewing thread
- Crochet hook 4mm
- Wool needle
- Sewing kit

### Body

With yarn A, make 35 ch. Work in rows.

**Row 1** (RS) 1 dc into 2nd ch from hook, 1 dc into each foll ch = 34 dc
**Rows 2–30** 1 ch, 1 dc into each dc to end **Row 31** dc2tog, 1 dc into each foll dc to 2 dc before end of row, dc2tog = 32 dc **Rows 32–45** As row 31 = 4 dc

Turn on side, 1 dc into each of rows 45–1. Fasten off.

On the RS, re-join yarn A in 1st dc of row 1. 1 dc into each of rows 1–45. Fasten off.

### Top

With yarn A, make a magic ring.
Work in a spiral.

**Round 1** 8 dc into magic ring. Pull yarn to close ring.
**Round 2** 2 dc into each dc = 16 dc
**Round 3** *1 dc into next dc, 2 dc into foll dc*, rep 7 times from *to* = 24 dc
**Round 4** *1 dc into each of next 2 dc, 2 dc into foll dc*, rep 7 times from *to* = 32 dc **Round 5** *1 dc into each of next 3 dc, 2 dc into foll dc*, rep 7 times from *to* = 40 dc Work 1 ss into next dc to finish.
Cut yarn and fasten off.

### Top leaves
With yarn B, *21 ch, turn, 1 dc into 2nd ch from hook, 1 dc into each foll 19 ch*, rep 14 times from *to* , 1 ss into 1st ch of 1st foundation chain. Fasten off.

### Finishing
Sew in the threads on the WS.
Sew the zip between the long edges of the body, aligning the top of the zip with row 1. Close the base of the body. Sew row 1 of the body around the top section of the carrot. Sew the leaves to the centre of the top section.

Photos on pages 54 to 55

# The animal carry-all

## Materials
- Yarn 100% acrylic for crochet hook 3.5mm: 2 skeins red
- 90cm x 70cm (35½in x 27½in) red Vichy fabric
- 1 buckle, 20mm (¾in) wide
- Sewing thread
- Crochet hook 4mm
- Wool needle
- Sewing kit
- Iron

## Main part

### Bottom
Make 31 ch. Work in rows.

**Row 1** (RS) 1 dc into 2nd ch from hook, 1 dc into each dc to end = 30 dc
**Rows 2–20** 1 ch, 1 dc into each dc

## Sides

Turn. Continue in a spiral.
**Round 1** 1 ch, 1 dc into each 30 dc, 1 dc into the end of each of rows 20-1, 1 dc into each of 30 ch along foundation chain, 1 dc into end of each of rows 1-20 = 100 dc **Round 2** 1 dc into back loop of each dc
**Rounds 3–50** 1 dc into each dc to end
**Round 51** 1 ss into foll dc, 3 ch (= 1 tr), 1 tr into each foll dc, 1 ss at top of 3 ch = 100 tr

## Flap

Continue in rows
**Row 1** (RS) 1 ch, 1 dc into each of first 30 tr, turn = 30 dc **Rows 2–20** 1 ch, 1 dc into each 30 dc
**Row 21** dc2tog, 1 dc into each foll dc until 2 dc before end of row, dc2tog = 28 dc **Rows 22–28** As row 21 = 14 dc
Fasten off.
On RS, re-join yarn in 1st dc of row 1 of flap. 1 ch, 1 dc into each of rows 1–28, 1 dc into each 14 dc of row 28, 1 dc into each of rows 28–1 from other side of flap.
Fasten off.
Sew in the threads on the WS.

## Pockets (x2)

Make 23 ch. Work in rows.
**Row 1** (RS) 1 dc into 2nd ch from hook, 1 dc into each foll ch = 22 dc
**Rows 2–26** 1 ch, 1 dc into each dc to end
Fasten off.

Sew in the threads on the WS.

## Shoulder straps (x 2)

Make 81 ch. Work in rows.

**Row 1** (RS) 1 dc into 2nd ch from hook, 1 dc into each foll ch = 80 dc

**Rows 2–5** 1 ch, 1 dc into each dc to end

Fasten off.

Sew in the threads on the WS.

## Handle

Make 41 ch. Work in rows.

**Row 1** (RS) 1 dc into 2nd ch from hook, 1 dc into each foll ch = 40 dc

**Rows 2–4** 1 ch, 1 dc into each dc to end

Fasten off.

Sew in the threads on the WS.

## Tightening cord

Make 90cm (35.5in) long chain.

Sew in the threads on the WS.

## Lining

### Cutting the pieces

*Measure length and width of bottom of bag.* Cut a piece (piece A) in Vichy fabric measuring (length + 2cm/¾in) x (width + 2cm/¾in).

*Measure circumference and height of sides.* Cut a piece (piece B) in Vichy fabric measuring (circumference + 2 cm/½in) x (height + 1.5cm/½in).

*Measure width and height of flap.* Cut a piece (piece C) in Vichy fabric measuring (width + 1.5cm/½in) x (height + 1.7cm/1¹⁄₁₆in).

*Measure width and height of pocket.* Cut two pieces (pieces D) in Vichy fabric measuring (width + 2cm/¾in) x (height + 1.5cm/½in).

*Measure width and length of shoulder strap.* Cut two pieces (pieces E) in Vichy fabric measuring (width + 1.5cm/½in) x (length + 2cm/¾in).

*Measure width and length of handle.* Cut a pieces (piece F) in Vichy fabric measuring (width + 1.5cm/½in) x (length + 2cm/¾in).

## Sewing the pieces

### Bottom and walls

Fold piece B in two lengthwise, RS to RS. Sew the two widths together 1cm (⅜in) away from the edge to make a tube of fabric.

Pin one edge of the tube around piece A, RS to RS, with the tube's seam in the middle of one long side of piece A. Sew the seam with a 1cm (⅜in) seam allowance. Make a small notch in each corner (don't cut through the seam!) to allow the fabric to fold over on itself when turned right side out.

Fold 1cm (⅜in) of the tube's free edge towards the WS of the fabric and iron flat.

### Flap

Fold 1cm (⅜in) of the whole piece C towards the WS of the fabric and iron flat.

### Pockets

For each piece D, fold 1cm (⅜in) all around towards the WS of the fabric and iron flat. Place the two pieces D on crocheted pockets, WS to WS, aligning them at the base. Sew them in place with slip stitches.

### Shoulder straps

For each piece E, fold 1cm (⅜in) all around towards the WS of the fabric and iron flat. Place the two pieces E on crocheted shoulder straps, WS to WS, centring them horizontally. Sew them in place with slip stitches.

### Handle

Fold 1 cm (⅜in) of the whole piece F towards the WS of the fabric and iron flat. Place piece F on the crocheted handle, WS to WS, centring it horizontally. Sew them in place with slip stitches.

## Making up

Sew the pockets on the main part of the bag, aligning their base with the bottom of the bag, and their back edge with the beginning of the flap. Sew the shoulder straps on the main part of the bag, at the base of the row of trebles, aligned with the flap and at the base of the wall, next to the pockets.

Sew each of the handles on the main part of the bag, at the base of the row of trebles, spacing them out by 4 stitches, so they are horizontally centred on the back of the carry-all bag.

Slip the lining in Vichy fabric in the bag, WS to WS, aligning the vertical seam of the wall with the centre of the flap. Sew the top edge of the wall with slip stitches. Pin piece C on the flap, WS to WS, aligning it with the base of the wall lining. Sew it using slip stitches.

### Finishing

Fix the clasp: the tongue part of the clasp on the last row of flap, centred, and the buckle part opposite on the front of the bag.

Weave the tightening cord between the trebles of the wall's last round so that the two ends come out in the middle of the front.

### Tip

For a sleek finish, make sure you accurately measure the crocheted parts and iron flat the fabric pieces. The fabric pieces' dimensions have been calculated to leave a small allowance along the visible edges of the crocheted pieces. Follow the order of making up.

# Bergère de France yarns used in these projects

| **The bear**<br>Photos on pp 14–17<br>Instructions on pp 66–67 | | **Yarn** | **Colour** |
| --- | --- | --- | --- |
| Body | | Norvège | **Duvet**<br>(Light Brown) |
| Jumper, shorts and hat | Yarn A | Barisienne | **Jardin**<br>(Light Green) |
| | Yarn B | Barisienne | **Amazonie**<br>(Dark Green) |
| Shoes | Yarn C | Barisienne | **Chicorée**<br>(Brown) |
| Backpack | Yarn D | Barisienne | **Châtaigne**<br>(Light Brown) |

*View a text version of this table*

| **The raccoon**<br>Photos on pp 18–21<br>Instructions on pp 68–69 | | **Yarn** | **Colour** |
| --- | --- | --- | --- |
| Body | Yarn A | Barisienne | **Titane** (Light Grey) |
| | Yarn B | Barisienne | **Réglisse** (Black) |
| | Yarn C | Barisienne | **Igloo** (White) |
| Overall | Yarn A | Câline | **Limaille**<br>(Medium Grey) |
| | Yarn B | Barisienne | **Vitrain** (Dark Grey) |
| Kerchief | Yarn C | Barisienne | **Geranium** (Red) |

*View a text version of this table*

| The fox | | Yarn | Colour |
|---|---|---|---|
| Photos on pp 22, 23, 27 Instructions on pp 70–71 | | | |
| Body | Yarn A | Barisienne | Orange |
| | Yarn B | Barisienne | Melisse (Off White) |
| | Yarn C | Barisienne | Réglisse (Black) |
| Suit | Yarn A | Barisienne | Tournesol (Yellow) |
| | Yarn B | Barisienne | Igloo (White) |
| Shoes | Yarn C | Barisienne | Epice (Brown) |

| The caribou | | Yarn | Colour |
|---|---|---|---|
| Photos on pp 24–27 Instructions on pp 72–73 | | | |
| Body | Yarn A | Norvège | Varech (Light Khaki) |
| | Yarn B | Norvège | Sapinière (Dark Khaki) |
| | Yarn C | Norvège | Rouet (Beige) |
| Jumper | Yarn A | Idéal | Calanque (Light Blue) |
| | Yarn B | Barisienne | Igloo (White) |
| Trousers | Yarn C | Barisienne | Marron (Chestnut) |
| Shoes | Yarn D | Barisienne | Châtaigne (Light Brown) |

| The wolf | | Yarn | Colour |
|---|---|---|---|
| Photos on pp 28–29 Instructions on pp 74–75 | | | |
| | Yarn A | Fourrure | Fouine (Medium Grey) |
| | Yarn B | Barisienne | Vitrain (Dark Grey) |

| The koala<br>Photos on pp 31, 32–34, 37<br>Instructions on pp 76–77 | | Yarn | Colour |
| --- | --- | --- | --- |
| Body | Yarn A | Norvège | Source (Grey) |
|  | Yarn B | Barisienne | Réglisse (Black) |
| Blouse | Yarn A | Barisienne | Méthylène (Turquoise) |
|  | Yarn B | Barisienne | Melisse (Off White) |
| Trousers | Yarn C | Barisienne | Pilote (Navy Blue) |
| Scarf | Yarn D | Barisienne | Geranium (Red) |
| Boots | Yarn E | Barisienne | Tournesol (Yellow) |
|  | Yarn B | Barisienne | Melisse (Off White) |

*View a text version of this table*

| The panda<br>Photos on pp 31, 34–36<br>Instructions on pp 78–79 | | Yarn | Colour |
| --- | --- | --- | --- |
| Body | Yarn A | Norvège | Glaçon (Cream) |
|  | Yarn B | Barisienne | Melisse (Off White) |
| Dress, hat and boots | Yarn A | Barisienne | Melisse (Off White) |
|  | Yarn B | Barisienne | Nérine (Dark Pink) |

*View a text version of this table*

| Three little pigs<br>Photos on pp 38–47<br>Instructions on pp 80–85 | | Yarn | Colour |
|---|---|---|---|
| Chef | Yarn A | Barisienne | **Guimauve** (Pink) |
| Butcher | Yarn B | Barisienne | **Rêverie** (Light Pink) |
| Junior chef | Yarn C | Idéal | **Nérine** (Dark Pink) |
| Chef's clothing | Yarn A | Barisienne | **Igloo** (White) |
| | Yarn B | Barisienne | **Réglisse** (Black) |
| Butcher's clothing | | Barisienne | **Igloo** (White) |
| Junior chef's clothing | | Barisienne | **Clapotis** (Blue) |
| Leg of lamb | Yarn A | Norvège | **Glaçon** (Cream) |
| | Yarn B | Norvège | **Rouet** (Beige) |
| | Yarn C | Norvège | **Viking** (Dark Red) |
| Sausages | Yarn D | Barisienne | **Nérine** (Dark Pink) |
| Roast | Yarn A | Barisienne | **Geranium** (Red) |
| | Yarn B | Barisienne | **Igloo** (White) |

*View a text version of this table*

| The bunny<br>Photos on pp 49–51, 53<br>Instructions on pp 86–89 | | Yarn | Colour |
|---|---|---|---|
| Body | | Barisienne | **Melisse** (Off White) |
| Clothes and basket | | Barisienne | **Guimauve** (Pink) |
| Ice cream cone | Yarn A | Norvège | **Rouet** (Beige) |
| | Yarn B | Barisienne | **Tournesol** (Yellow) |

*View a text version of this table*

| The baby rabbit  Photos on pp 50–53  Instructions on pp 92–93 | | Yarn | Colour |
|---|---|---|---|
| Body | Yarn A | Barisienne | Melisse (Off White) |
|  | Yarn B | Barisienne | Guimauve (Pink) |
| Hat |  | Barisienne | Guimauve (Pink) |
| Carrot-crib | Yarn A | Barisienne | Carotte (Orange) |
|  | Yarn B | Barisienne | Jardin (Green) |

*View a text version of this table*

| The backpack  Photos on pp 54–55  Instructions on pp 82–83 | Yarn | Colour |
|---|---|---|
|  | Barisienne | Geranium (Red) |

*View a text version of this table*

# Tables

| The bear | | Yarn | Colour |
|---|---|---|---|
| **Photos on** pp 14–17 | | | |
| **Instructions on** pp 66–67 | | | |
| Body | | Norvège | **Duvet** (Light Brown) |
| Jumper, shorts and hat | Yarn A | Barisienne | **Jardin** (Light Green) |
| | Yarn B | Barisienne | **Amazonie** (Dark Green) |
| Shoes | Yarn C | Barisienne | **Chicorée** (`Brown) |
| Backpack | Yarn D | Barisienne | **Châtaigne** (`Light Brown) |

*Return to main text*

| The raccoon | | Yarn | Colour |
|---|---|---|---|
| **Photos on** pp 18–21 | | | |
| **Instructions on** pp 68–69 | | | |
| Body | Yarn A | Barisienne | **Titane** (Light Grey) |
| | Yarn B | Barisienne | **Réglisse** (Black) |
| | Yarn C | Barisienne | **Igloo** (White) |
| Overall | Yarn A | Câline | **Limaille** (Medium Grey) |
| | Yarn B | Barisienne | **Vitrain** (Dark Grey) |
| Kerchief | Yarn C | Barisienne | **Geranium** (Red) |

*Return to main text*

| The fox | | Yarn | Colour |
|---|---|---|---|
| **Photos on** pp 22, 23, 27 | | | |
| **Instructions on** pp 70–71 | | | |
| Body | Yarn A | Barisienne | **Orange** |
| | Yarn B | Barisienne | **Melisse** (Off White) |
| | Yarn C | Barisienne | **Réglisse** (Black) |

| Suit  | Yarn A | Barisienne | **Tournesol** (Yellow) |
|---|---|---|---|
|       | Yarn B | Barisienne | **Igloo** (White) |
| Shoes | Yarn C | Barisienne | **Epice** (Brown) |

*Return to main text*

| **The caribou** | | Yarn | Colour |
|---|---|---|---|
| **Photos on** pp 24–27 | | | |
| **Instructions on** pp 72–73 | | | |
| Body | Yarn A | Norvège | **Varech** (Light Khaki) |
|      | Yarn B | Norvège | **Sapinière** (Dark Khaki) |
|      | Yarn C | Norvège | **Rouet** (Beige) |
| Jumper | Yarn A | Idéal | **Calanque** (Light Blue) |
|        | Yarn B | Barisienne | **Igloo** (White) |
| Trousers | Yarn C | Barisienne | **Marron** (`Chestnut) |
| Shoes | Yarn D | Barisienne | **Châtaigne** (`Light Brown) |

*Return to main text*

| **The wolf** | | Yarn | Colour |
|---|---|---|---|
| **Photos on** pp 28–29 | | | |
| **Instructions on** pp 74–75 | | | |
| | Yarn A | Fourrure | **Fouine** (Medium Grey) |
| | Yarn B | Barisienne | **Vitrain** (Dark Grey) |

*Return to main text*

| **The koala** | | Yarn | Colour |
|---|---|---|---|
| **Photos on** pp 31, 32–34, 37 | | | |
| **Instructions on** pp 76–77 | | | |
| Body | Yarn A | Norvège | **Source** (Grey) |
|      | Yarn B | Barisienne | **Réglisse** (Black) |
| Blouse | Yarn A | Barisienne | **Méthylène** (Turquoise) |
|        | Yarn B | Barisienne | **Melisse** (Off White) |

| | | | |
|---|---|---|---|
| Trousers | Yarn C | Barisienne | **Pilote** (Navy Blue) |
| Scarf | Yarn D | Barisienne | **Geranium** (Red) |
| Boots | Yarn E | Barisienne | **Tournesol** (Yellow) |
| | Yarn B | Barisienne | **Melisse** (Off White) |

*Return to main text*

| The panda | | Yarn | Colour |
|---|---|---|---|
| **Photos on** pp 31, 34–36 | | | |
| **Instructions on** pp 78–79 | | | |
| Body | Yarn A | Norvège | **Glaçon** (Cream) |
| | Yarn B | Barisienne | **Melisse** (Off White) |
| Dress, hat and boots | Yarn A | Barisienne | **Melisse** (Off White) |
| | Yarn B | Barisienne | **Nérine** (Dark Pink) |

*Return to main text*

| Three little pigs | | Yarn | Colour |
|---|---|---|---|
| **Photos on** pp 38–47 | | | |
| **Instructions on** pp 80–85 | | | |
| Chef | Yarn A | Barisienne | **Guimauve** (Pink) |
| Butcher | Yarn B | Barisienne | **Rêverie** (Light Pink) |
| Junior chef | Yarn C | Idéal | **Nérine** (Dark Pink) |
| Chef's clothing | Yarn A | Barisienne | **Igloo** (White) |
| | Yarn B | Barisienne | **Réglisse** (Black) |
| Butcher's clothing | | Barisienne | **Igloo** (White) |
| Junior chef's clothing | | Barisienne | **Clapotis** (Blue) |
| Leg of lamb | Yarn A | Norvège | **Glaçon** (Cream) |
| | Yarn B | Norvège | **Rouet** (Beige) |
| | Yarn C | Norvège | **Viking** (Dark Red) |
| Sausages | Yarn D | Barisienne | **Nérine** (Dark Pink) |
| Roast | Yarn A | Barisienne | **Geranium** (Red) |
| | Yarn B | Barisienne | **Igloo** (White) |

*Return to main text*

| The bunny | | Yarn | Colour |
|---|---|---|---|
| **Photos on** pp 49–51, 53 | | | |
| **Instructions on** pp 86–89 | | | |
| Body | | Barisienne | **Melisse** (Off White) |
| Clothes and basket | | Barisienne | **Guimauve** (Pink) |
| Ice cream cone | Yarn A | Norvège | **Rouet** (Beige) |
| | Yarn B | Barisienne | **Tournesol** (Yellow) |

*Return to main text*

| The baby rabbit | | Yarn | Colour |
|---|---|---|---|
| **Photos on** pp 50–53 | | | |
| **Instructions on** pp 92–93 | | | |
| Body | Yarn A | Barisienne | **Melisse** (Off White) |
| | Yarn B | Barisienne | **Guimauve** (Pink) |
| Hat | | Barisienne | **Guimauve** (Pink) |
| Carrot-crib | Yarn A | Barisienne | **Carotte** (Orange) |
| | Yarn B | Barisienne | **Jardin** (Green) |

*Return to main text*

| The backpack | Yarn | Colour |
|---|---|---|
| **Photos on** pp 54–55 | | |
| **Instructions on** pp 82–83 | | |
| | Barisienne | **Geranium** (Red) |

*Return to main text*

Printed in Poland
by Amazon Fulfillment
Poland Sp. z o.o., Wrocław